DELIVERING TRAINING

Suzy Siddons

Suzy Siddons specialises in the psychology of communication. After working for a West London Psychological Service and spending several years as a full-time writer, she entered the information technology industry as a training officer – this was the easiest way to get a free word processor! One and a half years later she was headhunted by a large computer manufacturer to join its sales training department, initially to set up and run training for their network of dealers and distributors, and later to deliver and originate courses for the sales, marketing, support services and field services divisions of the company. These courses covered a wide range of behavioural and business skills. Since founding her own training company in 1987 she has worked with a wide range of clients, consulting and training in the behavioural skills needed in business.

The only route to a professional career in personnel and development is through the achievement of the IPD's Professional Standards. The TRAINING ESSENTIALS series targets two parts of the process: Core Personnel and Development; and the four generalist modules in Employee Resourcing, Reward, Relations and Development (or their N/SVQ Level 4 equivalent). Whether you are seeking to qualify through college-based study, flexible learning or competence assessment, these texts will provide both essential underpinning knowledge and a comprehensive framework for learning.

Other titles in the series include:

Cultivating Self-development David Megginson and Vivien Whitaker

Designing Training Alison Hardingham

Developing Learning Materials Jacqui Gough

Evaluating Training Peter Bramley

Identifying Training Needs Tom Boydell and Malcolm Leary

Introduction to Training Penny Hackett

The Institute of Personnel and Development is the leading publisher of books and reports for personnel and training professionals and students and for all those concerned with the effective management and development of people at work. For full details of all our titles please telephone the Publishing Department on 0181 263 3387.

TRAINING ESSENTIALS

DELIVERING TRAINING

Suzy Siddons

INSTITUTE OF PERSONNEL AND DEVELOPMENT

Design and typesetting by Paperweight
Printed in Great Britain by
The Cromwell Press, Wiltshire

British Library Cataloguing in Publication Data
A catalogue record for this book is available from the
British Library

ISBN
0-85292-668-5

INSTITUTE OF PERSONNEL
AND DEVELOPMENT

IPD House, Camp Road, London SW19 4UX
Tel.: 0181 971 9000   Fax: 0181 263 3333
Registered office as above. Registered Charity No. 1038333.
A company limited by guarantee. Registered in England No. 2931892.

Contents

Dedication

This book is dedicated to my husband, David Nickson, and to our cat, Bonzo – my inspiration.

Acknowledgements

This book would not have been possible without the constant encouragement and help of my editor at IPD, Anne Cordwent. I would also like to thank Rhiannon Chapman of Plaudit, Richard Grimes of the Learning Unit at Rank Xerox, Andy Read, David Smith and Graham Baldwin of Reflex UK Ltd., Pete Thorn of the Enstone Flying Club and last, but not least, my husband, David, who put up with the agonies of having a writing wife.

Introduction

I love delivering training. It fulfils for me the five criteria for the perfect job – challenge, interest, variety, usefulness and discipline. Over the many years that this activity has been my way of life I have trained thousands of business people in a variety of behavioural skills using a variety of training methodologies, and each time I start a course it is another voyage of discovery.

I believe that there are several golden rules in training:

I Never make assumptions.

I Never over-train.

I Base all your training on reality and real working practices.

I Structure your courses carefully.

I Lead firmly at the start of a course.

Another essential point – and I did not know this when I started – is that practically all participants like to learn and it is up to the trainer to find the best way to make this happen.

It would be impossible to cover all the aspects of training delivery within this book, so I shall leave it up to you to find out how to operate a video camera, write on a flip chart, mend an overhead projector and the many other practical tasks that trainers undoubtedly need to perform in the course of their work. What we have concentrated on here is the underlying knowledge and behavioural skills that a trainer needs to deliver a compelling and effective training course.

1

Your Attitude to Training

The Shorter Oxford English Dictionary defines training in several ways:

> to treat so as to bring to the proper or desired form; spec. in Gardening, to manage (a plant or branch) so as to cause it to grow in some desired form or direction esp. against a wall, or upon a trellis or the like

> to instruct and discipline generally, to educate, rear, bring up

> to instruct and discipline in or for some particular art, profession, occupation, or practice

> to discipline and instruct (an animal) so as to make it obedient to orders or capable of performing tricks

> to undergo or follow a course of instruction and discipline.

So what are we – gardeners, instructors, disciplinarians, lion tamers, teachers or what?

Some personal definitions

Rhiannon Chapman, ex-director of the Industrial Society and managing director of 'Plaudit', defined the role of the trainer in business as follows.

> 'the trainer must have a specific end in sight, working towards achieving a specific result... [and] must create the right kind of learning environment so that participants get the opportunity to do the right kind of learning to achieve the stated objectives.'

Richard Grimes, head of the Learning Institute at Rank Xerox, succinctly defined a trainer as:

'someone who facilitates learning.'

A group of project managers actually being trained in negotiation and communication skills gave the following definitions of a trainer.

Andy Read, sales and marketing director of Reflex UK Ltd., said:

'someone who puts us in a situation so we can learn.'

Graham Baldwin, senior project manager at the same company, said:

'a reliable source of knowledge who helps us to learn.'

David Smith, another project manager for Reflex, said:

'someone who helps us to understand, who makes sense out of the theories.'

My personal definition is all of the above with one important addition:

'a trainer must be a super-effective multi-tasker with eyes in the back and sides of the head.'

The trainer as facilitator

The thread that links all these definitions is the one of 'facilitation'. The trainer's role is above all: to help learning to happen, to create an environment and atmosphere that encourages the learning process; to organise and present information in such a way that the participants can utilise it to increase their knowledge base; to organise and present activities that will reinforce the learning process; and to check and re-check that learning is taking place.

The hats trainers wear

To become facilitators we trainers must wear a wardrobeful of hats and fulfil a portfolio of functions – social secretary, information giver, motivator, educational specialist, presenter, quality controller, chairperson, mediator and business controller.

Social secretary

Here the trainer encourages the group to work together (see Chapter 4), ensures that the participants know at all times what to expect and looks after the logistics. The trainer also selects and organises the groups for group activities, looks after latecomers, introduces visitors, co-ordinates the course with the venue, handles mealtimes and coffee breaks and makes sure that any social activities associated with the course are successful. This last function is particularly important on residential courses.

Information giver and source of expertise

In technical training, where the participants are trying to acquire a clearly defined set of skills to operate machinery or technology, the technical knowledge and expertise of the trainer is crucial. It is perhaps less so on personal skills courses where the trainer is expected to know about the subject in depth but is not expected to have had experience, for example, of being a managing director or a chairman of a company. However, it is dangerous to train at a level right on the edge of your knowledge base or experience – someone will always ask the question that you should know the answer to but don't! Many skills trainers train people in far more senior positions than their own; it is the breadth of the trainers' experience and their ability to organise information and exercises that is valued here.

Motivator, encourager and inspirer

It is up to the trainer to set the pace and generate enthusiasm on the course. When participants encounter new skills, problems and behaviours they are often understandably cautious about exposing themselves to possible failure – careful handling of this caution is an essential skill for the trainer. Over years of assessing course critiques I have noticed that courses highly rated by the participants very often carry comments such as – 'The trainer's enthusiasm made the course enjoyable, and successful.'

Educational specialist

As trainers, it is not just enough for us to know our subject. We also need to consider the actual processes of learning, how people remember, how to reinforce new input, how to interpret complex information and how to help the participants internalise and make sense of the new. A trainer needs to be perpetually on the look-out for signs of understanding, misunderstanding, confusion, interest, lack of interest, uncertainty and irritation – and know how to act accordingly (see Chapter 5).

Presenter

It stands to reason that trainers who deliver presentation and public speaking skills courses need to have exceptional presentation skills themselves – do as you would be done by. But are these skills as essential for technical, management, business and personal skills trainers too? I think so. One of the prime attributes that all trainers need is authority. This is not the 'do as you're told' authority often wielded in the schoolroom, but the calm confidence that shows that trainers know what they are doing, can guide the course forward confidently, can resolve problems, can express themselves clearly and can 'think on their feet'. All these qualities are shown (or sadly, not shown) in the way the trainer presents information and handles the training room. Here the essential skills of clear, compelling and logical delivery, presentation of useful visual aids, question-handling skills and 'audience control' cannot be overlooked. Almost all trainers have nerves before a course

(I know I do – even after 20 years) but thankfully experience has taught us that these will pass within a few minutes and that *everyone* improves with practice. As a result, most trainers become effective presenters simply by doing their jobs.

Quality controller and disciplinarian

A trainer must keep discipline – not in the sense of a lion tamer, curbing the participants and controlling their actions, but also in the sense of keeping the course to time, applying a rigorous set of standards to the quality of the work produced on the course, giving clear feedback that highlights excellence and discourages the participants from taking 'the easy way out'.

If the training we deliver is to be perceived as worthwhile, then the same quality controls should be applied to training as they are to the goods or services a company manufactures or supplies. The trainer sets the tenor of the course. Sloppy thinking, careless tasking, poor time-keeping, over-aggressive or over-passive behaviours will all occur if the trainer allows it.

Chairperson

Even the driest of technical courses should have a large element of interaction in it. Certainly personal and business skills courses are mainly interactive – that is what makes them valid. When you have a roomful of intelligent adults interacting effectively, the trainer needs to take off the 'information giver' hat and become the chairperson – drawing everyone out, summarising what has been said, keeping to the agenda and timescales.

Mediator, referee and peacekeeper

Training courses often bring out the best in people, but there are also times when they seem to be an excuse for grandstanding, getting out the soapbox, settling private scores and generally behaving in a way that would be unthinkable in the office. Of course this may be one of the strengths of training courses – unfinished business can be uncovered which would otherwise remain unspoken. However, training courses are not therapy sessions and what might be a fascinating exposition of personal grievances to one participant is probably of little interest to the rest of the course (except as a spectator sport). The trainer needs to assemble a battery of skills and practices that allow him/her to defuse conflict; to have a set of safety mechanisms that protect the participants from each other (and sometimes themselves); and to keep their head when all about are losing theirs.

Business controller

Training is a business activity and therefore subject to the same constraints as any business. It should support the company objectives, it should give value for money, it should improve the performance of the participants, it should act as a generator of future success and it should stay within budget! The trainer should bear this in mind at all times.

The hats trainers should not wear

It is also certain that trainers should leave some hats in the closet. Trainers are not there savagely to criticise, to punish, demotivate or manipulate. And, although there should be an element of entertainment in all courses, we trainers are not there solely to amuse. Everything that happens on a training course should lead to an improvement in business performance. Here are some of the hats that are not becoming to trainers: the deity, the soliloquiser, the company spy and the infant teacher.

The deity

Trainers wearing this hat like to feel that they are indispensable and that without them people will go seriously astray. They act as if they are the ultimate and unquestionable source of all information – the giver of tablets of stone, the arbiter of all behaviours, the punisher of the unworthy, the giver of life. They often try to create dependency in the participants, a particularly silly thing to do when the whole purpose of a training course is to make the participants autonomous so that they can perform better when the training course is over.

The soliloquiser

This seems to be a hangover from the days when the formal lecture was the main method of getting information across. Trainers who rely on this role dislike participation – they probably feel that they would lose control if they let the participants speak. Sadly, this is an ineffective method for true learning when used too exhaustively. Adults learn best when they are allowed to experiment with new information (see Chapter 5), and having to sit and listen without interaction does not allow this. This is not to say that there is no place for the lecture in a training course. Listening to an expert is undoubtedly revealing, but this is only a part of the learning process and should be diluted by sessions that allow participants to make the information real to them as individuals.

The undercover agent and company spy

Without an atmosphere of trust it is very difficult to encourage participants to experiment with new skills where they may feel exposed to failure. Need I say more?

The schoolteacher – particularly the infant school teacher

Business training is not a schoolroom, where teacher always knows best and there are rules designed to control a large number of relatively inexperienced youngsters. Again, from long experience with course feedback, one of the most negative comments that a participant can make about a trainer is 'the trainer talked down to us', or 'the trainer treated us as if we were incapable of thinking for ourselves'. There are two incontrovertible facts that face every business trainer: the participants are at least as intelligent as you; and inexperience is not the same as inability.

Training versus teaching

Let us look further at the difference between training and the conventional view of teaching. The teacher/pupil relationship is one that we and all the people we train are very familiar with from our childhood – indeed, one of the expectations that participants often bring to a training course is that it will be like a 'lesson', that the training venue is nothing but a thinly disguised schoolroom and that the trainer is 'Miss' or 'Sir' without the mortar board.

Nothing could be further from the truth. Business training is (or should be) a voluntary activity. Trainees are adults in search of extra skills, understandings, methodologies, hints, tips and advice, chances to experiment safely – and a host of other experiences that will add to their business acumen and performance. They are also highly competent people in their own right with a set of relevant skills and experiences that already exist.

Lessons often end in a test or exam. Training courses rarely do, unless they are for a professional qualification. The outcomes of a training course may not be apparent for many weeks, and often simply cannot be assessed by a paper and pencil exercise.

Prescriptive training – why some participants ask for this

Undoubtedly some course participants will want you to be prescriptive – to give them hard answers and recipes. People often find it easy to cope with task-driven thinking where they are not expected to interpret what is presented on the course. Often they will push the trainer to give hard and fast answers because they feel that if they have a set of rules to follow they will know exactly where they are. As we said, their expectations of training are often based on their experience of directive training in the past. Indeed, the very subject matter of the course often dictates the role of the trainer – ultra-technical training demands clear instructions, fairly rule-bound exercises and exactitude of tasking. Training in personal skills such as communication, management, leadership and so on requires a much more exploratory approach. Here, hard and fast rules are little help. What is needed is a set of guidelines and exercises that allow the participant to discover for him/herself a methodology that will best suit his/her personality and the group within which he/she works, and enable him/her to cope with the inevitable changes that all businesses undergo.

Spurious power and the trainer

There is a strange phenomenon that sometimes occurs at the start of training courses. There the participants sit, possibly better qualified than you are, possibly out-earning you, certainly more experienced and knowledgeable about their business than you are, possibly higher up the corporate ladder than you will ever be; and yet they wait for you to tell them what to do, and what's more they very often do it at your bidding. What power! What influence! What a heady rush of adrenaline!

I call this the 'spurious authority of the felt pen holder syndrome', and it can be very seductive. It is an unwise trainer who believes in this power. We trainers have no power of detention, we cannot keep the participants in after school. We cannot write letters home to their parents and we cannot threaten to expel them; the cane is out as is the dunce's cap and the sarcastic put down. We have no head teacher we can send them to for a ticking off and we should stand them in the corner at our peril, for the dreadful truth is – *we* are the ones who are examined at the end of the course, and the power of the course critique is mightier than the trainer's felt pen.

Training beliefs questionnaires

Below are two little questionnaires. Answer as truthfully as you can; you may find the results enlightening.

Statement	Scoring			
1 Effective management can be helped by effective training. This is measurable and course critiques will prove this.	TOTALLY AGREE	PARTIALLY AGREE	PARTIALLY DISAGREE	TOTALLY DISAGREE
2 Training is a useful business activity, provided it sticks to safe subjects. Training does not seem to make much difference, but it can be a rewarding job.	TOTALLY AGREE	PARTIALLY AGREE	PARTIALLY DISAGREE	TOTALLY DISAGREE
3 Training could make an enormous difference to some people. Sadly, the very people it could benefit are the ones who don't come on the courses.	TOTALLY AGREE	PARTIALLY AGREE	PARTIALLY DISAGREE	TOTALLY DISAGREE
4 Training is an artificial activity that makes very little contribution to actual business. The real learning happens on the job.	TOTALLY AGREE	PARTIALLY AGREE	PARTIALLY DISAGREE	TOTALLY DISAGREE
5 Training is constantly changing. There are new methodologies always evolving that will one day make training the answer to most business problems.	TOTALLY AGREE	PARTIALLY AGREE	PARTIALLY DISAGREE	TOTALLY DISAGREE
6 Training should follow the needs of the organisation, step by step.	TOTALLY AGREE	PARTIALLY AGREE	PARTIALLY DISAGREE	TOTALLY DISAGREE
7 Trainers are the *éminences grises* of the organisation. They rarely make direct changes but have an influence throughout the organisation.	TOTALLY AGREE	PARTIALLY AGREE	PARTIALLY DISAGREE	TOTALLY DISAGREE
8 Effective training shows the company how to be more open and therefore more likely to achieve its objectives.	TOTALLY AGREE	PARTIALLY AGREE	PARTIALLY DISAGREE	TOTALLY DISAGREE

(continued opposite)

(continued from page 10)

Statement	Scoring			
9 Training is all about coping with change. It is not just about methodologies, it is about learning how changes can be made effectively.	TOTALLY AGREE	PARTIALLY AGREE	PARTIALLY DISAGREE	TOTALLY DISAGREE
	_____	_____	_____	_____

Interpretation of your stance as a trainer

Statement	Interpretation
1 Effective management can be helped by effective training. This is measurable and course critiques will prove this.	I am a teacher and my job is important. I can prove that there is nothing wrong with training. People do not realise how useful training is. One day the company will value my contribution.
2 Training is a useful business activity, provided it sticks to safe subjects. Training does not seem to make much difference, but it can be a rewarding job.	I am not prepared to take risks, I need to conserve my strength, it is a comfortable job if I do not expose myself too much.
3 Training could make an enormous difference to some people. Sadly, the very people it could benefit are the ones who don't come on the courses.	I am a real expert who could save everyone but I am not sure that the people who come on my courses actually deserve them or have the capacity to understand them. I can see what is going on even if others cannot.
4 Training is an artificial activity that makes very little contribution to actual business. The real learning happens on the job.	This job is pretty pointless. I should use my expertise elsewhere, there is not enough in training for me. I will probably leave.
5 Training is constantly changing. There are new methodologies always evolving that will one day make training the answer to most business problems.	I am the light in the wilderness, I could lead people to perfect business performance if only I could find the right methodology.

(continued overleaf)

(continued from page 11)

Statement	Interpretation
6 Training should follow the needs of the organisation, step by step.	Training is a reactive exercise and should only make changes that people will tolerate. It is not the job of the training department to lead change. Change can only be accomplished slowly, but it can be accomplished.
7 Trainers are the *éminences grises* of the organisation. They rarely make direct changes but have an influence throughout the organisation.	I am on to a good thing here.
8 Effective training shows the company how to be more open and therefore more likely to achieve its objectives.	Training needs to explore how we can make the people in the company work together more effectively. We need constantly to find ways to improve performance.
9 Training is all about coping with change. It is not just about methodologies, it is about learning how changes can be made effectively.	Training and trainers are agents of change, even though we may not know exactly how we do it. We must make things happen and integrate what we learn with how the company performs.

I suspect that we are all a mixture of the above attitudes, but some are healthier than others. A high agreement with attitudes 2, 3 and 4 may indicate a certain amount of 'burn out', where the trainer needs to re-evaluate his or her role in relation to the company strategies; 5 may indicate a zeal that may be out of touch with the gritty reality of everyday business life and 7 is perhaps a little self-seeking!

Who is your customer?

So far we have talked about the trainer, but trainers cannot train without course participants. Who exactly are we training? Are the people we train the same as the people who commission the course? Where does the trainer's loyalty lie and what factors should be taken into consideration? Who are our customers? Indeed, what is a customer?

Here is a list of possible customers:

- the managing director of a small company who needs training in public speaking for himself
- the head of personnel in a large UK company who wants training for her personnel staff of 24 on interviewing skills
- a freelance consultant who wants training (which he will personally pay for) on implementing ISO standards
- the manager of a group of secretaries who needs to bring her people up to speed on a new word-processing package
- the engineering manager of a manufacturer of wooden articles who needs to train his lathe operators on how to use their new lathes
- the graduate recruitment manager in a public services company who needs a course for his engineering graduates that will help them during their interview for chartered engineering qualifications
- the training director of a multinational chemical company who wants to implement a company-wide set of courses on project management
- the director of a training company who wants you to deliver its standard course on assertion skills.

All these are your customers in one way or another. The thing that they all have in common is that they pay your fees, even if they do not actually attend the training course. They are also the primary clients who will determine the type of course they need and therefore must be consulted while the training course is being designed and then debriefed after the training course.

The information you can gain from these primary clients will make a huge difference to the success or failure of the course. This information ranges from company objectives, departmental objectives, individual objectives and so on, to profiles of people who will attend the training, to background information on existing skills and needs, to future plans. Just because a primary client will not attend the actual course does not mean that he or she does not have an influence on the course itself.

The needs of primary clients

A trainer's loyalty lies first to these primary clients. They are the people who have the overall view of what they expect the course to do and where it fits into the development of their organisation. They will judge the success of the course not only on the individual value that the participants reported but on whether the required skills, practices, methodologies and individual increases in knowledge actually benefit the company as a whole, and whether the training has reinforced the standards, values and future plans that have been worked out at strategic level.

An analogy that might be useful here is that of the interior decorators who are brought in to turn your house or flat into a palace of beauty. Whereas you would undoubtedly take their advice about how things might look, it is unlikely that you would give them total freedom to organise and change things without reference to your needs and preferences. So it is with the trainer – you are working towards the strategic objectives of the primary client.

Once the training course is under way you will have a different set of customers.

Here is a list of possible customers at this stage:

▪ an 18-year-old office junior who is joining a course of experienced office workers for communication training

▪ a group of project managers attending a course on project evaluation and review technique charting and project management/manager tools

▪ five researchers from a pharmaceutical company attending a course on technical presentations

▪ seven PAs attending a course on accurate minute-taking

■ a 40-year-old manager attending a course on spoken Italian

■ the marketing department of an IT company attending a team-building session

■ a senior trainer from the Home Office attending a 'Train the Trainer' seminar

■ a completely mixed group from all sectors of different industries attending a public course on basic management skills

■ two sales account managers attending a course on financial skills for salespeople

■ a database operator attending a course on database management.

Each of these people is your customer, too, and may have a set of objectives for the course that is quite different from those of the primary client. They will also have different needs during the course, but they all share one thing in common: they want real value from the course in personal terms – particular skills, knowledge, confidence and insights.

A trainer's loyalty also lies with these more immediate customers, but it is important to bear in mind that the training course must fit with the overall business need, even if the course participants may not totally agree with this. It is part of a trainer's skill that he or she should be able to relate all the activities on the course to this overall business need.

Who are you training?

This may seem a redundant question bearing in mind what I have said about your customers in the last few paragraphs, but actually it is a serious question that needs to be addressed. Are you training the people as private individuals? Are you training them as if they are only what their job title describes? Are you training them as members of a group or department or overall company? We need to train them as all of these, and we need to find out as much was we can about them. The next chapter discusses just what you need to know about your customers.

Why are you training them?

Why are *you* training them? What made the primary client choose *you* as the trainer? Trainer credibility rests on many things, not just your ability to deliver well or handle the hurly-burly of the course. What expertise do you possess? What experience have you had? What is your track record? Who have you met who is a recognised guru? Everything you have done in your past business life is grist to the mill in making you a confident trainer. Have you been in the same sort of situations as your participants? Can you remember how difficult it was for you to acquire new skills and competencies? Do you have knowledge of different market areas, different industries, different job areas? Do you have anecdotes that realistically illustrate the subject you are talking about? I recommend that every trainer should prepare a short résumé (as adaptable as possible) that can be used as 'street cred' when meeting a new group of participants. This is not boasting – it is just the same as looking at a supplier's portfolio of past triumphs and achievements. It gives the participants confidence in your ability to run the course.

In brief

▍ Trainers multi-task the whole time, swinging between many roles. It is this ability to wear a number of hats that will make our courses successful.

▍ We need to look at the courses we run as part of the wider business picture not just as a 'spot fix' for a specific problem or lack of skills.

▍ The power of a good trainer rests in the ability to facilitate learning. We should encourage a learning environment where each individual in the extraordinary mix we are bound to meet on our courses can develop new skills and insights into the way he or she works within his or her company.

2

What You Need to Know Before You Start to Train

This chapter covers the information that a trainer needs at the start of a course. It covers three main areas: information about the company commissioning the course, information about the participants themselves and information about the course itself. No matter how well structured the course or how carefully you have followed the briefing from the primary client, this pre-information is vital to your success.

The value of pre-course knowledge

There is a tale that trainers often use about the value of knowledge: after a £4,000,000 refit, a luxury cruise liner once developed a rattle that resonated throughout the first-class decks. The liner's owners knew that this would drive the passengers mad (particularly the ones who had paid thousands of pounds for their tickets), and called in specialists to strip down the engines, the air conditioning and everything else that might have caused the rattle. To no avail, the rattle continued. Finally the world's greatest expert on rattles was called in. He walked around the ship for only 10 minutes, then he took a small hammer from his pocket and, with great precision, tapped once with his hammer on an obscure piece of piping. The rattle immediately stopped, never to recur again. Two weeks later, he sent in an invoice for £10,000. The chairman of the shipping line was aghast at the cost and immediately asked the world's greatest expert on rattles to itemise and justify the invoice. The world's greatest expert on rattles replied by return of post. This is what he wrote:

To tapping with the hammer   £1
To knowing where to tap   £9,999.

We may not be the world's greatest expert on rattles, but we can and should become expert about the things that will affect our training courses. To do this we need to do considerable research before each and every course that we deliver.

Omit this research at your peril – not only is poor preparation a recipe for disaster on the course, but research has shown that one of the main causes of nerves before appearing in front of an audience is a feeling of unpreparedness and not knowing what to expect.

In a perfect world we would have time to research every single factor that might affect a course, our briefing from our clients would be detailed and insightful and we would be able to speak to all the participants in person before the course started. We would always train in the same locations (which would be perfectly appointed) and we would be familiar with all the companies sending participants to the training session. The world is not perfect, so here is an overview of the areas of information you need to gather in order to plan the successful delivery of any course. Some information is needed before the course actually starts, other information can be investigated in the early stages of the course.

The company

Whether you are delivering training to a group of people who all work in the same company or to a group of people from different companies, you need to know the company background of each of the participants. After the course they will be putting their new knowledge and skills into practice within their company surroundings so there must be no mismatch between what they have learned and the working actuality of their environment. As an example, I once attended a 'Train The Trainer' course along with a group of trainers from several other companies. We were a really mixed bunch. There was a trainer from the motor industry who trained assembly line workers, there were two trainers from a high-tech computer manufacturer, one a management skills trainer and the other a technical trainer, there were trainers from the banking world, trainers from a hairdressing school and a trainer from a video production company. We were all on the same course – but our companies had very different needs. The course facilitator had really done her homework. Where the course covered highly structured learning needs that applied to the sort of training the motor industry and technical trainers needed, she illustrated how it would be used in the manufacturing industry. Where the course covered more general and widely applicable ways of training, she used the service industries as a model. We all left the course feeling that what we had learned was highly relevant to each of us – even though as a group we had all covered the same agenda.

Let us look at some of the areas we need to investigate.

Company priorities

It is absolutely crucial that you have a clear set of objectives for the course from the primary client. This is the starting-point for the course.

Both the primary client and the trainer need to know the answers to the following questions:

- Where does this training fit into overall company practices?
- Why is this training needed?
- What will follow this training course?

Overall company practices

This would be obvious in the case of technical training

where the course is necessary to enable the participants to do their job efficiently; it becomes more complex when looking at skills courses such as management skills, communication skills, quality management and so on – where the participants not only need to acquire the relevant skills, but also need to practise them within the norms of the company itself. (Norms are the behavioural standards that exist within a group; see Chapter 3.)

For instance, take leadership skills: what is the type of leadership practised within the company? Is it directive, participatory, remote, autocratic or democratic (to name but a few)? There is little point in encouraging behaviour on the course that simply would not work in practice. In fact this would be completely counterproductive, since the working reality would contradict everything learned on the course.

Even a subject seemingly as universal as presentation skills can fall into the reality trap. I do a set of presentation courses for an international manufacturer. The sales division makes a series of exciting, fairly long, highly visual sales presentations, full of anecdotes and benefits, encouraging interaction between the audience and the presenter. Consequently these are the factors we concentrate on in their presentation courses. On the other hand the finance division hates interaction, finds anecdotes and visual aids unnecessary, just wants the facts, presented briskly in a pragmatic manner – a case of make it short, make it clear and get off. Its presentation courses are a completely different matter, concentrating almost entirely on clarity of delivery, logical flow and structure.

The only way you can find out how the company is going to use the skills you are training (and therefore the specific skills you should be focusing on), is to research company practices before you deliver the course. Discuss these issues with the primary client. If possible, wander about, interview a selection of potential participants, talk to the human resources division. The course can then be tailored to what really happens, not what should happen. Case studies should always reflect actuality, otherwise they are nothing more than an exercise in imagination. This point was forcibly brought home to me once on a negotiation course. We had decided to use an imaginary case study to illustrate the stages in preparing for a negotiation. It was beautifully constructed to bring in all the factors that might affect a really complex negotiation, based on several areas such as bulk discounts, delivery costs, plant rental costs, exchange rates and so on. 'Splendid', I thought, 'this will really make them think.' It did indeed. The participants were commissioning editors who worked for a publishing company, and they only ever dealt with single authors – not much need for bulk discounts there! They found the whole exercise unnecessary and tedious. Certainly they understood the reason for exploring all the factors involved in a negotiation, but they had no knowledge of the minutiae of manufacturing negotiations – and, what is more, no need for that knowledge. The golden rule for all exercises, role plays and case studies is: *make it as real as possible*.

Why is this training needed?

Because the participants need new information or skills?

Because they need to change existing working practices?

Because they need to correct personal faults?

Because they need re-motivating?

Because they have asked for it?

Because everyone else has been on a training course and they might feel left out?

Because it is part of an ongoing development plan?

You need to find out not only why they think they are being trained, but also why the primary client thinks they are being trained (the two may not be the same) and tailor the course accordingly.

What will follow this training course?

Training never exists in a vacuum. That said, there are sometimes occasions when people attend courses to learn skills that they may not put fully into practice until a later date. If this is so, then the trainer should make sure that the participants take away exercises or activities that will allow them to revise or integrate their new skills while they are waiting to use them. For example, management training may often be given before the participant actually becomes a manager, perhaps as part of a development programme; activities such as observing the success or failure of existing management practices, planning what they would do in specific situations, reading selected articles or books, or finding a mentor will keep the new skills fresh.

Participant information

There are four main areas to consider here:

■ straightforward personal details like name, age, location and so on

■ individual objectives and expectations

■ job-specific information

■ background information on existing skill sets and experiences.

You also need to investigate preferred thinking and learning styles and personality factors like priorities and patterns of behaviour. These last factors are covered in Chapter 4 where we consider the ways in which adults learn.

Straightforward personal details
Name

Obviously you need to know this if you are going to prepare name cards and personalise the course handouts, a helpful thing to do if you are using workbooks or manuals which all look the same, as it allows each person quickly to identify their own course material. It is also a real help if you can memorise the list of names before you actually meet the participants – this makes it easier to link names to faces at the start of the course.

Age

This is not as important as the name, but a useful piece of information when you are deciding on working groups. You may want to distribute the more experienced people around the groups, rather than find that they are all together in one group.

Location and contact numbers

Apart from the possibility that you may need to contact participants either before or after the course, this is useful information in logistical terms – how long a journey will they have had to the training venue? Might they need to get away promptly on the last day?

Individual objectives and expectations

Personal objectives for the course

If possible, you need to find out in advance what each individual personally wants from the course. To provide this information participants will need to have a fair idea of what is going to happen on the course. An agenda and list of main course objectives should be sent out with the pre-course material.

Personal objectives may be quite different to course objectives. For example, a course objective may be: 'to be able to enter data into a database accurately and retrieve the information when needed.' Whereas a personal objective might be: 'to overcome my fear of computers', or 'to compare the ease of use of database A with database B.'

Setting individual objectives really makes each participant focus on exactly what they want out of the course. It encourages the process of active learning and listening and makes the course personal to each participant. This, above everything else, will ensure the success of the learning experience.

Personal expectations

These are a potential minefield. Many of us are familiar with the participant who is attending the course under duress or who has heard from others about a 'similar' course that was perhaps not as successful as it should have been. As trainers we often have no control over who is sent on our courses, or how their expectations have been set, and as a consequence we have to cope with negative expectations that are potentially damaging to the running of a course. If you know in advance what participants' expectations are likely to be or what their attitude is to the course then you can take any necessary remedial action early on in the course before faulty expectations warp the participants' perception of the whole thing. I find this is a major concern in courses concerned with personal skills like assertion training, time management and communication skills. Unwilling participation in these courses is very hard to handle since there often seems to be implicit criticism from the manager in sending people to the course in the first place such as 'your assertion skills are not good enough', or 'your communication skills are not up to scratch'. Little wonder then that the participant feels uncomfortable at the start of the course.

It is always worth asking the primary client how they chose the course participants and how they presented the course to them. If there seems the slightest likelihood of any feelings of duress in the participants then you need to allow extra time in the course introduction to clear up these expectations and turn them from negative to positive. For example, in the case of an assertion course, instead of introducing the course as 'how to become more assertive personally' (thereby reinforcing the unspoken message 'you are not assertive enough'), try to present the course as providing tools and techniques to handle people within your work group who are passive or aggressive.

When I first started training adults I ran (amongst other things) a course for PAs on word processing (this was a long time ago and computers were then machines of mystery and incomprehensible technology). Most of the senior PAs who came to be trained were in their forties and some were very alarmed by the prospect of having to learn a complete set of new skills. Although they were aware that the ability to handle a word processor rather than just a typewriter was becoming a vital business skill, they still felt 'put upon' and, sadly, many of them had not been consulted before being sent on the course. Naturally they felt resentful, nervous and worried. The first two times I ran this course I could not help but notice that there was a chilly feeling to the opening session. Over the first coffee break, when the ice had been broken and the participants were feeling happier about the course, the truth came out. If I had known this before they arrived, I would have included a reassurance session and would have made sure that their expectations were very carefully set from the very first time we started the courses.

Job-specific information

Armed with the information you have researched about the company you now need to look at the participant's role within the company.

Job title

This is essential. It gives you valuable insight into the areas that will be of concern to them, what their priorities are in terms of applying the information acquired on the course, and who else on the course is likely to have shared experiences.

The participant's manager

Here we move into the sometimes murky area of reporting course results. It is perfectly reasonable for the commissioning manager to want to find out how his or her people did on the course. The danger is, however, that the participants may feel wary about secret reports going to the manager. I get round this by making it a cardinal rule that anything that will be said or reported to any manager is first communicated to the participant concerned – and make a point of saying this at the beginning of the course.

It is also possible that you may already know the manager and this gives you the chance to ask him or her how the participant feels about attending the course.

People reporting to the individual participants

It is particularly important to know if the participants will be applying what they learn on the course to themselves, or whether they will be both learning individual skills and having to pass these skills on to the people they manage. If the second is the case, then it would be useful to build into the exercises or role plays some of the skills needed to pass the new learning on. Also, those participants with a large number of people reporting to them have different problems to the lone wolf who only has to concern himself or herself with the application of new skills.

Number of years in this position and in the company, previous jobs

You will need to know just how experienced each participant is at his or her particular job. This makes an enormous difference to the amount of background material that is needed to bring everyone up to roughly the same level of basic knowledge. As an example of this, I was asked to run a course for seven project managers working in the chemical industry. Five of them had been project managers for over five years and were obviously very familiar with the company methodology used for running projects (the course was all about contingency planning and risk analysis). However, two of them were not only new to project management but also new to the company.

This was quite a problem. Somehow the inexperienced had to be brought up to speed in terms of basic project-management skills and company methodologies, or a large amount of time would have to be spent during the course teaching the grandmothers to suck eggs while the newcomers were given the basics.

We got round this problem by sending the two newcomers on a company induction course and providing pre-course workbooks and literature on basic project-management concepts. The work groups were carefully chosen and briefed so that for each exercise every newcomer had a mentor (an experienced colleague willing to help and advise). In the event, this was very successful because the mentors told me afterwards that by having to explain the basics they had deepened their knowledge and understanding of the processes that they had come to take for granted. It also led to a particularly successful exercise in team bonding.

Imagine, though, what you as a trainer would have felt if you had discovered this state of affairs only on the first day of the course. 'Thinking on your feet' would have taken on a whole new meaning!

Main responsibilities/concerns (in their current job)

This information will be useful to you when deciding how to focus the participants on using their newly acquired skills. Your role plays and exercises should be based around these responsibilities and concerns – for example, if you are delivering a course on time management and you know that the participants have particular trouble with efficient telephone handling, you can use the situation of telephone communication as a background for role plays. Another example – if you are delivering a course on word processing and you know that the participants have expressed a concern about how to write letters, then each of the exercises you use could illustrate good practice in constructing letters, even though the actual exercises were designed to teach how to format text or how to do a mail merge and so on.

Qualifications/courses attended directly relating to their current job

This information will help you to pitch the course at the right level – it will save you from the cardinal sin of presenting information that participants already know as if it is new to them (something that drives calm and happy course members into a frenzy).

Anyone they really should not sit next to or be with for group working

You could always ask participants to choose who they would like to sit next to from the list of participants (this should always be sent out with the course joining instructions), or leave namecards on a side table and let them sit where they like as they come in on the first day. However, you will need to have teams organised for group working and role-play exercises. If this is the case, then send out the proposed team lists in the joining instructions, with a note asking participants to let you know if they would like to change teams.

Participants' skills and experience

As mentioned before, there is nothing more exasperating than going on a course where you have to sit through session after session containing information you already know or teaching skills you already possess. If the course material demands that everyone must work at roughly the same speed and at roughly the same knowledge level (for instance in technical training, physical skills training or induction courses), then you will need to know the basic skill and knowledge level of each participant. This can be done with a pre-course questionnaire (make sure you get it back at least a week before the course). Where you have two or three people who are more skilled than the rest you will need to devise extra exercises to keep them busy while bringing the rest up to speed.

Where the course is about softer, more individual skills such as interviewing, managing people, giving presentations, training skills, selling skills and so on, people improve their skills incrementally from their own base level. A common skill level is not so necessary for the learning to take place.

The course itself
The venue

This may seem obvious, but it is very disconcerting to arrive at the course venue and find that the room is unsuitable, that you do not know where the telephones are or who to contact for refreshments, photocopying and all the other necessities that make a course run smoothly. If you cannot visit the venue before the start of the course, then make sure that you arrive early enough. When using a new venue, arrive at least one and a half hours before the scheduled start of the course to iron out any problems. Appendix B contains checklists to help with the logistics of this.

The course materials

You need to be thoroughly familiar with all the course documentation and to have worked out how to introduce it. Explaining to the group how the documentation is laid out and how to use it may seem a very minor point, but unless the participants know where glossaries of terms are, where the exercises are documented, whether there is an index, which parts of the documentation to use and when, and whether there are any documentary conventions (such as having an overview first, then detailed information, then exercises and then a checklist), they are unlikely to use the course materials effectively. It is a small housekeeping point, but one well worth the short time needed to cover it.

In Brief

▮ The more a trainer can prepare participants for a course, the higher the prospect of success for that course.

▮ The more the trainer knows about the participants, the more that course can be tailored to fit their needs. When expectations have been correctly set, where the trainer is aware of each and every participant's objectives, backgrounds, fears, hopes and past experiences, then the likelihood of the course achieving all its objectives is extremely high.

▮ A pre-prepared questionnaire covering most of this vital information should be sent to the participants at least three weeks before the course starts. Ask that the completed questionnaires be returned to you a week before the start of the course so that you can make any adjustments needed without rushing. Appendix A shows an example of a pre-course questionnaire.

▮ Preparing for a course is a little like cooking from a recipe – if you do not know what the ingredients are, then all the sophisticated culinary techniques in the world will not produce a great meal.

3

The Reality of
Leading a Course

'I must follow them, I am their leader .'

Andrew Bonar Law.

'The real leader has no need to lead, he is content to point the way .'

Henry Miller.

'The final test of a leader is that he leaves behind him in other men the conviction and the will to carry on .'

Walter Lippmann.

This chapter looks at leadership behaviour on training courses, the group dynamics affecting any collection of people coming together with a common purpose, the roles that are needed within a group to keep the group healthy and what can happen if the group becomes smug or complacent.

Leadership

Do training groups need a leader? If they do, why do they need leaders? What are the consequences of not having a leader? What does a leader actually do? What skills does a leader need? Is it possible to train and lead at the same time? Does our expertise as trainers make us natural leaders? When should we lead and when should we train? Why do some people on courses try to take over from the leader or trainer?

These are difficult questions for the trainer, as well as difficult questions for the participants. To try to answer some of these questions, I offer the following story:

Last year a friend of ours went on holiday to Italy. The tour took in Rome, Siena (which she had never visited) and Florence (which she knows very well). There were qualified guides to show the tourists the treasures of each city and a charming courier who stayed with them throughout the holiday.

An itinerary was sent to her two weeks before she was due to leave, with a detailed breakdown of all the places and artworks that they were going to visit and a list of available lectures and seminars to be held in the hotels in which they would stay. She had a great time underlining all the things that really interested her, putting question marks by the things she was less sure about, and crossing out the things she did not intend to spend time on – after all, it was her holiday and she had paid a lot of money for it.

The tour started in London where the courier met the group, introduced herself, and started everyone talking to each other. After about half an hour, when everyone seemed comfortable with each other, she quickly and efficiently told them what was going to happen on the journey to Italy.

My friend told us afterwards: 'From the moment we met in London I knew that the tour was well organised, so I could relax and look forward to seeing and hearing about all the things that interested me.' The flight was comfortable, the pilot was chatty and the landing was perfect. They found the coach and the courier without any trouble and drove to the hotel. Again, everything was organised with a view to the tourists' comfort.

The two days in Rome were a great success and on the third day they set off for Florence, where my friend was not particularly interested in going out with the rest of the group because there were several paintings she wanted to look at that were not in the mainstream tours. The courier noticed this and organised a packed lunch for her and a friend who was spending the day with her.

And so the tour continued, the courier kept everyone going, sorted out any problems, looked after the travelling and hotels, the visiting experts shared their knowledge, the group shared information and newly discovered art treasures. She told us: 'It was one of the best tours I've ever had – I learned what I wanted to learn and saw what I wanted to see – and more, because there were so many knowledgeable people in the group. I could choose for myself as well as joining in. It met all my expectations. I knew where I was and how to get help if I needed it. I shall use the same company again next year, so long as we have the same courier – she was brilliant.'

Who were the leaders, trainers, experts and guides in that tour? The courier? The airline pilot? The visiting experts? Other members of the group? My friend? In truth they *all* were at one time or other. And so it is on a course. Leadership swings round to the most appropriate person at the time. There must be, however, one constant – the courier, the person who facilitates the whole journey. This is, particularly at the start of the course, the primary role of the trainer. Without leadership at this point, the trainees' journey may not even start.

The contract between the trainer and the group

The course leader/facilitator/trainer and the course participants need to make an agreement at the start of the course. It could be put like this: 'as a trainer I'll do everything *I* can do to make learning possible on this course if you will agree to do everything *you* can to learn.'

The first thing that the trainer has to do to make this learning possible is visibly to lead the course. To do this effectively you must first look and sound like a leader. This means making a conscious effort to look calm, welcoming and in control. Most of all, never let the participants arrive at a course without someone (preferably the trainer) being there to welcome them. This gives the impression that the course is out of control, that the training organisation does not know or even care what it is doing, and that the trainer does not care about the welfare of the group. It may also mean that you as a trainer feel flustered and this will surely show in your body language, not a good start to the learning contract.

Without a leader the group goes nowhere. There are, however, several types of leadership and several different leadership behaviours that need to occur.

Initial leadership

This is essential when the group is in the pre-forming confusion stage (see page 40). Here the leader (almost always the trainer, although occasionally a commissioning manager might take this role) tells the group what to expect, makes the introductions, copes with the logistics and generally sorts out the basic necessities for the course. Trainers should not worry whether the course participants like them at this point; what is needed most is a clear definition of why the group has come together and what is expected of them, both individually and as a group. Chapter 4 looks in detail at how to run the opening sessions of a course.

Tasking

This is one of the most important duties of the trainer, and one that many trainers have the most difficulty with. Chapter 6 contains recipes for tasking certain types of training activities. All leaders must be able to set clear tasks for the group, particularly when the group is immature – this is nothing to do with the age of its members, but all to do with how well the group performs *as a group*. Groups mature as time passes, and as this happens the leader should do less and less tasking, allowing the group to develop internal tasking skills. Bearing in mind the fact that most training courses cram a great deal of activity into a short time frame, it is essential that from the start of the course the setting of tasks must be done in a systematic manner.

Here is the basic recipe for setting clear tasks:

- state the objectives of the task
- define exactly who is involved in the task
- define the steps needed to complete the task
- set the time frames
- set the location
- distribute any materials needed
- check that the group have understood what they are being asked to do.

Setting a pattern to the way tasks are defined gives the participants a template for individual activities and encourages them to keep to time schedules.

Energising

A successful course can be characterised by the amount of energy that the participants put into the tasks they are asked to do on a course. Enthusiasm on the part of the trainer will energise the participants. Trainers who allow their enthusiasm for their subject to show are much more likely to make the participants enthusiastic. If you look at the course assessments of particularly successful courses you will very often find the comment: 'the trainer was enthusiastic and really kept the course going.'

Speaking a little faster, using powerful and positive words and body language makes the participants approach new course modules with anticipation; an essential part of active learning. This is particularly needed during the 'dead hour', the short period after lunch when almost everyone needs encouragement to stay awake.

The very nature of training rooms – body heat from the number of people, often with artificial lighting, very often without windows that open, with recycled air and ambient background noise – is enough to send people to sleep at the best of times, so the trainer must allow for this and take every opportunity to re-energise the participants. Short breaks, stretching exercises and activities that make people move around will all help to keep attention and energy levels as high as possible. They should be built into the structure of the course.

Decision making

Like tasking, decision making is an essential leadership action when the group is immature. However, a good leader needs to back off when the group is sufficiently confident to make its own decisions. Failure to do this stultifies the group, making them dependent on the trainer and unlikely to perform well when the trainer is not there to decide for them.

Motivation

This is probably the most important leadership action that the trainer performs, and an activity that needs to be done constantly throughout the course. What is it that motivates people? Success, tough goals, rewards, praise, peer pressure, personal goals, praise from the trainer, fair criticism, problem solving, feedback from the rest of the course, self-feedback from video or audio tapes, gold stars, packets of sweets? Any or all of these might be appropriate. Certainly the trainer should keep a continual check on how close the course is coming to achieving the general and personal objectives. This is an inherent part of personal motivation.

Delegation

Essentially, delegation is handing a task over to someone else. If only it was so simple! True delegation takes time and effort if it is to be successful. There are times when it is necessary to delegate tasks on a training course, for example, leading 'break-out' groups where the course leader simply cannot be in two places at once. To do this effectively you need to prime the delegatee *before* the course, since the time needed is quite considerable.

What you should not delegate:

▪ rewards
▪ tasks that only you as course leader can do – for example, giving out certificates or course prizes
▪ strategic tasks
▪ tasks to do with the objectives and policies – for example, setting course objectives and standards or course timing
▪ evaluation tasks
▪ discipline (keeping the course in order), praise, resolution of conflicts, performance evaluation
▪ confidential information.

If by delegating a task you have to reveal confidential information, think very carefully about whether the delegatee should be in possession of this information.

Delegation is an important leadership activity. Without it you may lose focus on the things on which you really should be concentrating. One word of warning, though: delegate as much as possible to your backup team – course administrator, logistics manager for the venue and so on; but think very carefully about delegating to course participants if you feel that the tasks you delegate to them may interrupt their learning.

Giving feedback

The rules for successful feedback are covered in Chapter 6. Feedback is one of the most efficient ways of reinforcing learning, particularly feedback from the trainer who is seen as the expert. Lack of feedback undermines success, even in people who feel that they are doing well. If a participant has to ask how he or she is doing, this is a sign that they need more feedback and reinforcement.

Rewarding

When participants do well, when they have obviously gained a new skill, do not keep quiet about it. Feed back their success, pointing out specifically the behaviours that were successful. This is very necessary on courses involving personal skills, where lack of confidence makes people hesitant.

Correcting

Not all feedback is positive, there will be times when you have to point out behaviours or procedures that are not successful. Do not be afraid to do this: the participants really want to know how to correct faults, or may not even be aware that they are making them. Remember, though, to discuss only the behaviours observed and never make personal value judgements. Be absolutely specific and only comment on things that really can be changed.

Mediating

Undoubtedly there will be times when disagreements and conflicts may arise within the group. While this is healthy and should be encouraged there may be times when you feel that this is getting out of hand – for example, when personal disagreements between participants seem to be unfruitful, or two opposing camps disagree so much that it holds up the efficient running of the course. Here you must mediate and take control back. Not to do so will cause the conflicts to escalate. Remind the combatants that the course has a limited duration and that, while they have every right to their opinion, it would be better to continue with the course than spend the whole time covering what is, after all, just a small part of it. Be even-handed and try to resolve the conflict during a break time.

How groups bond together

As a trainer you are not only responsible for communicating the contents of the course, the actual learning modules. You are also responsible for the logistics of the course. You will run a more effective course if you understand the way people behave when they are part of a group. Group dynamics looks at the behaviours you can expect from people within a group. These behaviours can often be quite predictable so it is useful for the trainer to know what to expect.

Very few training courses require the participants to work as isolated individuals; yet often individual course participants may never have worked with the other participants as a group. They may be from the same company, but from different divisions of that company, they may even be from different companies and market areas, even different cultures, yet they have all come to the same course. In order for a course to be successful it is important that the participants bond as a group, sharing their ideas and skills and interacting in role plays and discussions. These bonding behaviours can be expected at the start of any course.

Initial confusion

No matter how carefully you have set expectations for the course, there are likely to be problems at the start. Usually the participants are not totally familiar with their surroundings, they are not likely to know everyone in the room, have never seen the course documentation before, may not know the trainer, may not know (or may have forgotten) exactly what is going to happen to them during the course. They will be somewhat confused and even a little apprehensive. This point in group formation is where clear direction must be set by the trainer: the individuals have not bonded as a group yet and unless the trainer gives then a common direction, they never will.

These are some of the questions they will be asking:

- ▮ *What are the objectives of the course?* Why am I here? What am I trying to achieve?
- ▮ *Where is everything situated?* Where are the lavatories, where will we be having coffee, lunch and tea? If the course is residential, where is my room? Where do I have my evening meals?
- ▮ *What are the time scales?* When will the course end? What time does the course start after lunch, coffee and tea breaks?
- ▮ *What are we going to cover?* What is the agenda? Will we be videotaped? Will there be evening work?
- ▮ *Who else is on the course?* Do I know anyone? Does anyone else have the same concerns as me? Are there any conflicts of interest? Can I trust the trainer?

No matter how confident each participant might be in normal circumstances, it will take a little while for each of them to feel quite comfortable. This is the 'pre-bonding' stage in group formation. The participants mill around, trying to get answers to as many questions as possible. Do not expect them to be particularly friendly to you, the trainer, or to others on the course. At this point they are in need of clear objectives and expectations. Here the trainer is acting very much like the courier at the start of a journey.

Forming into a group

Once participants have a common direction they can begin to get to know each other and start to come together as a group or set of sub-groups. The trainer at this point needs to act as a genial host, introducing the participants to each other, letting them talk to each other, encouraging them to find shared objectives and needs. This is the 'forming' stage in group development.

Stormy weather

It is at this point that a strange thing often happens. There may be a direct challenge to the trainer's authority. Almost certainly there will be a certain amount of jousting for position, where each group member tries to work out where they are within the 'power structure' of the group. This is not surprising: each participant has a certain identified status within his or her working group, and this may not be the same as their position within the course group. For example, a senior manager, used to leading his or her team, may find himself or herself in the unfamiliar position of having to follow the lead of the trainer, or a participant used to following the lead of a manager may suddenly find that he or she is in the position of having more expertise than the person who manages him or her. This switch in role takes a little getting used to, and while this is happening a certain amount of 'storming' can be expected. An experienced trainer will allow this to happen. The internal pecking order of the group needs to be sorted out by the group itself.

Setting up group norms

Now that the hierarchies within the group are identified (by the way these may well change as the course progresses), the group needs to work out the unspoken rules that will allow them to work comfortably together. These unspoken rules, or 'norms', arise quite rapidly. Norms such as timeliness, openness, disclosiveness and friendliness are set early on, often arising from the behaviour of the trainer. Other norms such as willingness to experiment and formality or informality may come from existing company norms. Wherever they come from, the group will need to establish its own set of rules.

Now that these three stages, pre-formation confusion, forming and storming are past, the group is ready to perform.

Roles within the group

It is the nature of groups that people within them take on certain roles that are needed to keep a group healthy. All members of a group perform two types of activity: task activity and maintenance activity.

Task activities in training courses

These are the activities necessary to make the learning happen: joining in an exercise, filling in a checksheet, making a presentation, answering questions, asking questions, taking a test. These activities have a measurable outcome and are a part of the course sessions.

Maintenance activities within the group

These activities help to maintain the smooth working of the group and are not necessarily part of the course sessions. In fact, they often go on in the background all the time that the group is together. Under this heading come behaviours like: leading the group, helping the leader (whoever that may be), finding resources for the group, acting as devil's advocate (someone who takes up an opposing position for the sake of argument), checking the accuracy of the group's observations, energising the group, acting as mediator when conflict occurs and a host of other actions that help make it possible for the group to cohere.

Major roles within the group

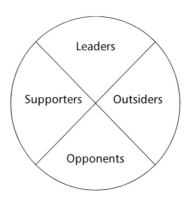

These four roles occur in all balanced teams. If any of these is missing the team will malfunction. Individuals within the group may take on one or more of these roles, often changing quickly from one to the other as the team requires this. Having already looked at leadership (see page 32), let us look at each of the other roles in turn.

Opponents

Where you have a leader, you also have opponents. For the inexperienced trainer this may seem alarming – the very idea of participants rebelling against the leader seems frightening. But think about this. If the leader is completely unopposed you have a group of sheep, blindly following the shepherd. On a training course you need interaction, you need feedback on how individuals are learning, you need a healthy respect for the power of the individual. Opponents should be encouraged. Try questions like: 'can you think of another way of solving this problem?' Or: 'can you see anything that might cause difficulties with this process?'

These encourage members of the group to think things through for themselves instead of unconditionally accepting ideas without examining them. Of course there will be exceptions to this – if you have someone with a personal axe to grind that has nothing to do with the course then you should handle this 'off-line'.

Supporters

It is always pleasant to have supporters. It makes life easier: the supporters help to keep the course moving along, facilitate group interaction and are of immense help to the trainer. Encourage them, but not to the point where the group becomes so comfortable that its members concern themselves only with complete harmony and stop challenging and thinking for themselves.

Outsiders

These are often the most difficult for the trainer to handle. They seem to sit on the sidelines, critically observing what is going on and rarely joining in. This may be due to their basic personality or learning preferences: they may be happiest working alone and wary of showing inexperience. However, by taking the role of the observer they have a unique viewpoint that is essential to the health of the group. It is very easy to forge a group that is so strongly bonded and so energised by what it is doing on the training course that its members forget that the course is a part of a wider world; the outsiders can give valuable feedback on the relevance of what is happening in terms of outside reality.

Healthy groups

For a training group to be healthy, a trainer needs to encourage the four group roles, there needs to be a balance between task and maintenance activities and there should be a balance between enthusiastic acceptance and healthy scepticism. Opponents and outsiders are essential if the group is to relate the training to their real life and to their individual needs.

Group Think

This is a worrying bug that only seems to affect successful teams. It was identified in 1972 by behaviourists Janis and Mann. They observed a set of behaviours that occurred when teams perceived themselves as 'winners'. These behaviours led to the team becoming smug and careless (even though the team itself did not seem to be aware of this). The outcome of these behaviours was that the team carried merrily on, not checking the outcomes of their behaviours and finally became so inwardly congratulatory that they forgot the wider objectives of what they were doing. Sadly, this can be a real problem with successful training courses, so we need to watch out for it.

Group Think might occur:

- if the team is tightly bonded
- if the team never has criticism or feedback from the outside
- if there is a really strong and controlling leader
- if the team never looks for alternatives
- if the team fails to evaluate itself, and the progress it is making.

You need to take corrective action if you see any of the following things happening:

- Team members never doubt that there is consensus amongst themselves.
- Each participant thinks that everyone (except him or herself) is in agreement. Participants wrongly assume that because others have not disagreed verbally it means that everyone is happy.
- There is direct pressure on others to agree: any doubters are 'pooh-poohed' and urged to conform.
- One or two group members act as peace-keepers, trying to prevent doubters from raising problems.
- Group members believe that 'nothing can touch us, we're the best'. They often think that the group is beyond reproach and that external factors do not apply to *this* team.

How to cure Group Think

Be vigilant, keep checking that what you are doing on the course relates to the external world. Keep evaluating the validity of what course members are learning by looking at the following factors:

- Are there real gains and losses for the group if they follow Group Think behaviours?
- Are there real gains and losses for others outside the group that might stem from these behaviours?

∎ Would we feel comfortable about these behaviours in the real world?

∎ Would important people we are connected with think we were behaving appropriately?

If you have the feeling that your course participants are starting to suffer from Group Think then there are several actions that you should take.

∎ Encourage discussion: explore alternatives, check assumptions, do not let course members blindly accept what you or they say without questioning it.

∎ When the group appears to agree, directly ask them if their silence means agreement – and make sure that you get everyone's view.

∎ Make your leadership impartial.

∎ The leader should not state his or her position until everyone has spoken. By not giving his or her point of view and not suggesting a solution, the leader allows the rest of the group to develop ideas in an open atmosphere which will allow alternative ideas to emerge.

∎ Every member should evaluate himself or herself.

∎ Encourage the participants to express their doubts and objections freely.

∎ Play the devil's advocate. Give one or two members the task of opposing any majority verdict if it seems to be too easily accepted. Choose someone to take up an unpopular standpoint.

∎ Bring in an outside expert. The expert will not have been party to the pressures that have caused the Group Think and will bring a refreshing breath of fresh air to the discussions.

In brief

- As group leader the trainer has to be much more than just the purveyor of instructions and wisdom. If the group is not handled carefully learning will not take place. Never neglect 'housekeeping' or logistical chores – the smooth running of the course depends on them.

- Right from the start of the course firm leadership is essential. Not only must you fulfil the leadership behaviours but you must look and sound like a leader.

- When groups come together you need to help them through the form, storm, norm stages of group bonding.

- You can expect all four group roles to exist within your group of participants: leaders, supporters, opponents and outsiders; without these roles the course will not be successful.

- As the participants develop their group skills, you can begin to take a less directive leadership style, but you are still in charge of all the comfort factors of the course.

- Watch out for Group Think. This can turn a really successful course into a smug but closely bonded group of under-performers who have completely lost touch with reality.

4

Starting Up a Training Course

The start is arguably the most significant part of the course. Get it right and your chances of overall success are good. Get this stage wrong or hurry through it and you will have to spend a great deal of time and effort later in the course to make up for this. This chapter looks at the four elements of a good start: the logistics of a good start; introducing the course itself; getting to know the group; and finally, how to create and maintain a learning atmosphere.

The logistics of a good start

Let us start with the nitty gritty: logistics. It is true to say that if the participants are uncomfortable, the course will not be as successful as it might be. It is absolutely true to say that if the trainer is uncomfortable then the course will definitely be less successful than it might have been. As trainer you are in command of the training environment, so what comfort factors do we need to consider?

How to arrange the room

Here I am talking about training courses with between four and 30 participants, where the delivery method is not simply the lecture and the participants will be working sometimes in a large group and sometimes either individually or in smaller groups.

You need to consider all these things:

■ How close are the participants to each other? Too close, and they will feel that their space is being constantly invaded, particularly from behind. Too far, and they will feel disinclined to talk, discuss and interact.

■ How near is the trainer to the participants? Too close, and the trainer will feel obliged to project his or her voice less and may well feel uneasy standing when the rest of the group is sitting. Too far, and the trainer will have to project his or her voice too much and may feel isolated from the group. Think about the distance between a stage and the first rows of the stalls in a cinema or theatre and you will see what I mean.

Ideally, the trainer should test out preferred distances well before the participants arrive. Sit in the participants' places – have you enough elbow room, can you spread out the course documentation, can you push your chair back without bumping into the table behind? Stand in the trainer's space: are you towering over the front row, can you make gestures easily, can you move freely around the training space?

Now think about the equipment.

■ Can every participant see the flip charts, screens, white boards and demonstration area? It is amazing how many conference centres have the overhead projector immediately in front of the screen so that not only is the trainer likely to block the view but the projector itself is in the way.

■ Can you get to the flip chart/white board easily without having to edge past other furniture, trip over cables, push equipment out of the way?

■ Where are you going to put your course materials, slides, demonstration equipment, trainer's box and so on so that you can get at them easily?

■ Is the trainer's table in a position where you are forced to stand behind it instead of having the option of moving towards the participants?

■ Do you need an extra chair for the trainer to use while role-play exercises or participant presentation are going on?

■ If you are using cameras and monitors on the course, where should they be positioned, are all the cables covered or stuck down with masking tape? If not, why not?

■ Do you need 'break-out' rooms for small group exercises? Are they set up so that the participants can use them easily? Where are they?

■ Where is the nearest photocopier, telephone, fax?

■ Where are the facilities? Where will coffee and lunch be served, where can the participants park?

The list seems endless, but all these factors need to be under your control. If possible I send a layout plan to the venue before I arrive so that the people who look after the venue will know how I like it to be arranged (see Appendix B for venue checklists and plan). In any event you should arrive well before the course starts so that you can move things around to suit your needs and those of the course.

What you need to have ready

Obviously, you must have the course materials and the essential course equipment; but what about course cards which show the name of each participant? What about drinking water, pencils, extra flip charts and so on? A course checklist and details of essential trainer's 'extras' which I always carry on every course are given in Appendix B. Most of these points may seem obvious, but I know from bitter experience that it is often the little snags that cause the longest delays or interrupt the course far more than their importance merits.

Timing and pacing the start

There is one golden rule: never hurry the start of any course. Sadly, this is the time when the trainer is most nervous: there are all those new people to meet, so many things to think about, so many unknown factors. When we are nervous our heart rate accelerates, our breathing rate increases and we tend to move too quickly. This in turn makes us even more breathless and nervy. Slow down. You will look more in control, more believable and much more approachable. If the trainer is feeling apprehensive, then imagine how the participants are feeling. They too need time to adjust to their new surroundings and relax into the frame of mind that will make learning possible.

You should allow, at the very minimum, half an hour for the start of any course, even if the course is a short one of a day or less. You may need more time if the course is a long one, the group is large or if it is necessary for the group to be firmly bonded before any exercises begin.

Having said that it is important to slow yourself down in order to give the participants confidence in your ability to lead the course, you should paradoxically put as much energy into the start of a course as you can. You need to make a splendid first impression.

The importance of first impressions

The session is prepared, coffee, lunch and tea have been organised, you know who to expect, the kit is ready and working, the manuals are laid out, the training room looks lovely, you have covered every possible eventuality. Here comes the crunch – the participants are arriving.

You have 20 seconds to make a good first impression. That is all it takes for people to make up their minds about you; to decide whether or not they are going to like you, believe you, trust you, have fun, be bored, learn or rebel. It is not fair, is it?

Well, the spiffy training room, the obvious care and

professionalism with which you have prepared the venue and the handouts and the fact that the participants have had all that pre-session information will help. Hopefully, the manager you have been dealing with will have given you good reviews. But now it is up to you.

Body language

No matter how you are feeling, if you do the following things not only will you give the impression that you are in control, but you will actually feel better:

- *Make sure that you stand tall*. This has nothing to do with your height, more to do with the way you hold yourself. When we are nervous we tend to 'guard' ourselves, we tend to keep our upper arms tightly against our chest, or to hunch our shoulders. This is a perfectly natural thing to do, but it makes us look apologetic. So – straighten your back, look the world in the eye, think TALL. Look also in Appendix C for exercises to 'warm up' your voice and tips on projecting it.

- *Start with a smile*. But remember – too much smiling makes people think we are trying to please them too much. When people are communicating with you, listen carefully – there is no need to smile all the time, a nod or a thoughtful expression will pay far greater dividends than an ever-ready smile. Look also at the way people use their eyebrows. High-credibility people seem to have very slightly lifted eyebrows and look alert and interested.

- *Eye contact* is one of the most significant indicators of status and competence. It is noticeable that high-status, high-credibility people have a much higher eye-contact rate than anyone else. They are not afraid to look others straight in the eye, they do not keep their eyes cast down or look at the ceiling or floor when they are talking to others. Try to keep your eye contact up – people will trust you more, believe you more and know that you are interested in them. There is a significant difference between high eye contact and staring – we all know instinctively what this is and will look away if we feel we are making people uncomfortable or uneasy.

- *Watch your speed*. If you want to be taken seriously – do not hurry. A scampering, hasty, flustered person does not look as if he or she is in charge or capable of handling a course. Slow down, take things slowly. Confident people take their time – this is why policemen are trained never to run unless there is a real emergency. If you move too fast you will look as if you are hurrying to catch up – not as if you are doing the job competently. Also if you slow yourself down, you will give yourself time to think – a useful exercise when time is short and decisions should be made carefully. Since you, as a trainer, wish to give the impression of being totally in control this is most important right at the beginning. You can use speed later in the course to energise the group or give urgency – but not at the start. Start slow, speed up later.

- *Make the most of your space*. Throughout history, space has been one of the most powerful ways of defining power. Space is used to show the world what is powerful, who is powerful and who makes decisions. The more powerful you become, the more space you will be given – a bigger office, a bigger desk, a car parking space, a bigger house and so on. People will even stand further away from you to show their deference. It is said that when John F Kennedy became President of the United States he found that there suddenly seemed to be an invisible line on the carpet of his White House office which visitors were reluctant to cross. The way you handle your personal space tells people a great deal about how you feel about yourself.

Feelings of self-consciousness, shyness, uncertainty, dislike, fear and pain are shown by a withdrawn, minimised body posture and small inward moving gestures – usually with the palms of the hands hidden. Self-confidence, liking, wellbeing and happiness are all characterised by an expansive outgoing body image with expansive, outward moving, open-handed gestures.

As a trainer make the most of the fact that you 'own' the training room – do not limit yourself to the training table area. Move freely round. It will make you that much more powerful. This is why I give trainees a conducted tour of the training area – even though it may be on their premises!

Here is a summary of positive and negative body language.

POSITIVE	NEGATIVE
Friendly and co-operative	**Defensive**
Look at the other person's face, smile and occasionally nod as the other person is speaking	Don't look at the other person; avoid any eye contact and instantly look away when they look at you
Make open-handed gestures	Keep your hands closed
Do not cross your arms	Cross your arms
Occasionally touch your face	Constantly touch your face or rub an eye or an ear
If sitting, cross your legs towards the other person	If sitting cross your legs away from the other person
Lean towards the other person	Lean away from the other person
Move closer	Move away
Confident	**Worried**
Not much blinking	A great deal of blinking
Looking into the other's eyes	Licking or chewing your lips
Initiating the handshake	Keeping your hands hidden
Taking up a lot of space	Limiting your movement
Keep your hands away from your face	Keep touching your face; cover your mouth while talking
Sit calmly and comfortably	Wriggle about while sitting
Lean back a little while sitting. Stand calmly and still	Fidget with your feet

(continued on page 56)

(continued from page 55)

POSITIVE	NEGATIVE
Thoughtful	**Aggressive**
Listen to the other with your head slightly tilted	Stare aggressively; look over the top of your spectacles
Slowly stroke your chin	Point or make sharp gestures
Lean forward to speak	Stand when the other is seated
Stand still	Stride around
Lean back to listen	Loom over a seated person's shoulder; stand too close

Introducing the course itself

Having the course signposted at the entrance to the training venue is a start. Make sure that the participants know where the training room is. It is also a help to have a flip chart or overhead projector displaying a welcome message and the course and trainer's name actually in the training room. You would be surprised how many training centres are like anthills with bemused participants wandering in and out of training rooms trying to find out where they are supposed to be. If it is at all possible, I like to invite the participants to meet in the coffee lounge half an hour before the course starts so we can get to know each other informally. If this is not possible, welcome each participant as they arrive in the training room.

Start as promptly as possible. I say 'as possible' because the first day of a course is the one time where you can allow the start time to slip just a little – people may have had difficulty finding the venue, finding a parking place and so on on the first day. I say 'just a little' because more than a ten minutes wait is not fair on the people who have arrived promptly. If people arrive more than ten minutes late, pause the course and welcome them personally, do not expect them to slink in and find their place while being ignored. They will probably be embarrassed by being late, so try to help them through this embarrassment.

The formal start of the course

The pre-performance bells, the dimming of lights, the drawing back of the curtains all signal the start of a performance in the theatre. You need to signal the formal start of the course too. What do you need to cover?

Introducing yourself

Even if you have met the participants before the course, you need to introduce yourself formally as the course trainer. The participants may not be aware of your qualifications for delivering the course. Here you need to tell them who you are, what your (relevant) background is, what experience you have of the subject matter and any other 'street-credibility' factors that you think will give them confidence in your ability to deliver the course.

Course and company objectives

You have established the course and company objectives before the course and should have included these in the pre-course literature. They need to be re-stated here, put onto a flip chart sheet and prominently displayed throughout the course. You will be collecting personal objectives from the participants later. An explanation of why the course was judged to be necessary can also focus the participants on what you as a group are trying to achieve.

A set of objectives for a presentation skills course might look like this:

▮ to enable participants to give business presentations an effective structure

▮ to introduce a set of company standards for visual aids

▮ to identify personal strengths and weaknesses in presentation skills

▮ to practise the standard presentation scripts for the company's new insurance products

▮ to practise voice projection and clarity of speech

■   to practise the skills needed for a Master of Ceremonies.

The reasons for giving the training course might be:

■   The company is about to enter the finance market place with a new product for insurance companies.

■   This will necessitate road shows, seminars and conferences where the sales and marketing group will be presenting to potential customers.

Logistics

In order to feel comfortable, the participants need to know where everything is, what timescales are involved and what is likely to happen to them in logistical terms while they are on the course. This includes not just what will happen in the training room, but also what will happen in the venue and if necessary the locality. You also need to cover any legal requirements like confidentiality, safety issues, site rules and security issues. Do not forget to tell the participants about any message-taking, telephone and fax facilities that are available.

The agenda

Now show the participants the agenda – this, too, should have been sent out with the joining material. I put the agenda on a flip chart and stick it up on the wall and then talk them through each module, explaining (fairly generally) what is in each module, what it is for and how it fits into the overall course. By the way, the only timing information I put onto the agenda are the start, end and coffee, lunch and tea breaks. I do this deliberately, even if the course is one that runs like clockwork, because you can never be absolutely sure which modules will under- or overrun. Each group of participants is bound to be different and a module that one group might find easy and pick up rapidly might need much more time with a different group. If timings for each module are set in stone on the agenda this may lead to concern on the part of the participants that they are being short changed if it under-runs, or being forced to drag a session out if they have reached their goals before the allotted time.

Personal objectives

Only now can you ask the group to think about their personal objectives. Until they have heard exactly what is going to happen they cannot know which modules or skills will be of particular interest or use to them. As we said in Chapter 2, personal objectives may be very different from course or company objectives and they need to be much more specific.

Ask the participants to check their objectives with the S.M.A.R.T. Test. This little test is used by trainers for many things, not just objectives. Basically it tests whether objectives can be met, whether tasks can be achieved and whether information is likely to be easily assimilated.

This is how it works:

- the S stands for Specific
- the M stands for Measurable
- the A stands for Achievable
- the R stands for Relevant and Resources
- the T stands for Time-bound.

If their objectives are too complicated, break them down into smaller, simpler objectives. They should be able to express each objective in a simple sentence. For example, the objective: 'I want to improve my presentation skills' may sound like a simple sentence, but is in fact far too general. The question to ask here is 'Which presentation skills in particular?' which might be answered with: 'Well, I'd like to be more audible and crisper in my speech, and I'd like to handle my nervousness so it doesn't show.' Already the objective is much clearer and more specific.

Then ask them how they are going to know when they have achieved their objectives and how they will measure their success. Will they know they have succeeded by feedback from you and the group? Will they be able to observe their performance on video?

Now the participants need to consider whether their objectives are achievable at all. For instance, an objective like: 'I want to be the first man to break the two-minute mile' is quite specific and certainly measurable, but if looked at in the light of past human performance and the fact that the speaker has only one leg, fails the achievability test.

Now look at the relevance of the objective and the resources available to help you achieve the objective. How does this objective sit in the real world? How relevant is this course objective to the way you and your company work? There is little point in acquiring a skill on a course that you will never actually use again.

You also need to think about what help, information, skills, kit, space and so on will be needed. If these are not available then the objective does not make sense. For example, I once worked with a group of managers who wanted to train all their personnel to use a new piece of software. The objectives were specific – to achieve a working knowledge of software X; measurable – they had devised a set of excellent exercises and a final test; and achievable – other companies had trained their personnel on the same package. However, the available computers that could be used on the training course could not be configured to suit the software, so in resource terms this was an impossible objective.

Finally, ask them when they expect to achieve this objective. On the training course? After a period of practice? How long will they take? Ask the participants to write their objectives down at this point, you will be collecting them later.

Alison Hardingham's *Designing Training* in the *Training Essentials* series has an excellent chapter (Chapter 3) on setting course objectives.

Getting to know the group

Now the trainees should feel comfortable with you, the course and the territory, but how do they feel with each other? Sometimes they will know each other, sometimes they will not. Certainly you, the trainer, need to find out more about the participants' personalities, likes and dislikes and ways of working as quickly as possible. Getting the participants to introduce themselves helps you to do this.

Introduction exercises

There are many introductory techniques – some formal, some informal, some efficient but not too much fun, and some efficient and great fun. It is up to you to pick the one that you feel will be the best for the course. Before any introductions, get each participant to fill in a name card using large letters.

Standard introductions (about two minutes per participant). Formal

Each participant should stand up (where they are sitting, not in front of the class) and tell the rest of the group:

▮ name

▮ job title

▮ responsibilities

▮ brief background

▮ what he or she wants from the course.

You then write their objectives down on a flip chart, writing each person's name by his or her objectives. Stick the flip chart sheets on the wall.

The reverse interview (seven minutes per participant). Less formal

Pair the participants. Each one has to interview the other for three minutes and find out:

▮ name

▮ job title

■ responsibilities
■ brief background
■ what he or she wants from the course.

Each then presents what he or she has found out about his or her partner. Again, the trainer writes down the objectives on a flip chart.

This is a more successful start-up game since it is often easier to talk about someone else and affords opportunities for witticisms. It also gets the participants to know each other.

Picture this (five minutes per participant). Informal

Give each participant a flip chart sheet and a set of flip chart pens and ask each to draw a pictorial representation of the facts you need to know. It is important that the trainer should do his or hers first so that the trainees will know what is expected of them. The above facts should be illustrated.

Each person then explains what they have drawn. Again, the trainer either collects the course objectives from each trainee and writes them down, or asks the participants to write their objectives on their flip sheets and then sticks them up on the wall.

Colour, car, character (five minutes per participant). Very informal

Each participant is asked to pick a colour, a car and a character that represent their personalities. They each write them down and then read them out, explaining why they picked them. They then state their objectives.

For example: I would pick the colour gold because I want riches, value and to endure for ever. I would pick a large, 1920s Citroen with running boards because I like history, elegance, safety and style. I would pick Mozart because he was surrounded by music and made the world a happier place. Again, the trainer collects the course objectives from each trainee and writes them down.

Do not worry about the amount of time that this might take. A successful introductory session is worth its weight in gold and will repay you a hundred-fold when the course gets going.

What to look for during these introductions

While the personal introductions are going on, you need to be listening and looking carefully. The way people introduce themselves gives you valuable information that will help you during the course. Look for these things:

Behaviour Observed	Useful Information
Who volunteers first?	Probably feeling active, enthusiastic. May be a valuable ally for the trainer, probably willing to lead in other activities
Who hangs back?	Probably more reticent, quieter. May be taking the 'observer' role. Give this person extra time to join in. Do not push at the start. See if there are any problems about attending the course
Who talks about his/her private life?	Disclosive, probably likes to look at the people side of work and feels comfortable in an informal atmosphere
Who reveals nothing personal and talks only about the job?	Probably feeling pragmatic. Likes to get the tasks done but does not feel comfortable when asked to talk about feelings
Who took longest?	Maybe needs to talk in order to internalise information. Uses discussion to help learning
Who was quiet and hesitant?	This one may need encouragement to speak, but do not force it
Who has their arms tightly folded?	Investigate to see if there is a problem. (If the chairs have no arms this may not be a valid judgement)
Who is avidly reading the course manuals?	This person may like a lot of detailed information
Who does everyone look at after they have spoken?	This person may be influential or have power over the rest of the group. Find out!

Creating a learning atmosphere

Once you have introduced the course, the logistics and yourself and encouraged the participants to introduce themselves you are well on the way to creating a learning atmosphere. Now the participants need to focus themselves on the information that they will be dealing with. They need to listen pro-actively instead of reactively. Reactive or passive listening is what you do when the radio or television is muttering away in the background without anyone paying particular attention to it – rather like many business presentations I have had to attend. Pro-active or active listening is what you do when you have chosen a programme to listen to or watch, and which you are thoroughly interested in. At this point in the course introduction you can do two things to encourage pro-active listening and focused attention.

Introducing the course materials

First take the participants on a guided tour of the course materials. Show them the manual, point out how it is arranged and take them through the contents. If it is a workbook that they will write in, then encourage them to do so. Even if it is purely a reference manual, give out highlighter pens and encourage them to mark information that is of particular importance to them as it arises on the course.

Maintaining pro-active listening

Secondly ask them to think up at least three specific questions that they want the answers to during the course. Collect these on a flip-chart sheet with the questioner's name by each one, and stick it on the wall. As the answers come up over the duration of the course, point this out and tick the questions off. It is useful to do this at the start of each new course section.

When introducing each new speaker or course module you need to go through some of the same activities as when introducing the course. Obviously you do not have to go through the personal introductions each time but each new module must have its expectations set, its objectives stated and its importance and relevance pointed out – particularly if the module specifically achieves individual objectives or answers the questions of the participants (what is called in the trade – 'This one's for you, Joe').

Setting ground rules

As mentioned in Chapter 3, the group is at this point still coming together. Group norms will not yet be set, so you can help this process by setting some standards that will help you with the organisation of the course. Depending on the formality or informality of the course you can make these as serious or light-hearted as you think is appropriate. Certainly a word about punctuality is necessary here, as are safety rules if equipment is being used on the course.

On most courses, feedback is an essential part of the learning cycle, so feedback rules (see Chapter 5) should be stated here. If you already know the group and have a strong rapport with them you might like to extend this. I have a small metal dustbin which I call the 'sin bin' and I ask the group to make up a set of rules and the fines that will be levied for breaking them. Here is the list of rules that the last presentation course I gave came up with:

- lateness   2p per minute
- over-running on personal presentations 1p per minute
- falling asleep during presentations   10p
- boasting and lying   10p
- failure to volunteer   10p
- being nasty to the trainer   20p
- turning your back on the audience   10p
- invoking absent authority   10p
- jargon   10p per word
                                                             or per initial.

At the end of the course we had collected £5.40 which we sent to Children in Need.

In brief

- The ultimate success of a course is heavily dependent on how it starts. A clear, structured start where expectations and objectives are set encourages the participants to stay on track.

- Do not neglect the comfort factors that will make the course run smoothly for both the trainer and the participants.

- Creating rapport by getting to know the participants helps to bond the group and gives the trainer an opportunity to observe the behaviours of the participants.

- Active learning needs to be fostered throughout the course, but most particularly at the start of the course when the participants may lack focus.

- Information about the course, participants' objectives and questions should be written up and displayed throughout the course.

- Setting ground rules not only makes the course run smoothly, but also helps the group through the 'norming' stage in group behaviour.

5

Pacing a Course: How Adults Learn

Enter the trainer – a large pile of fat course manuals under one arm, twin carousels crammed with 35mm slides under the other. 'This will only take three hours', she says, 'so let's get on with it.' You can practically hear the collective sigh from the course participants who can see an interminable, static training session ahead of them.

Naturally you would never do this, but it is all too easy to overestimate the length of time that people are happy to sit still and listen – and indeed overestimate the amount of information that can be taken in at a single session. This is particularly so when the course is going well, when the participants are obviously enjoying themselves and the trainer feels that he/she could add extra value by expanding the course modules. Never confuse giving information with learning. Learning is a complex process requiring not just the receiving of information but the assimilation, integration and practice of new skills and attitudes.

Training should be entertaining, but this is not the same as a play or a film where the audience is happy to sit passively and be diverted for an hour or more at a time. If learning and change are to take place, the course must be delivered so that new ideas – ideas which at this point are a set of fairly abstract verbal or visual concepts – can be converted to understandable working information, patterns and habits.

How adults learn

This chapter looks at the basic facts about the way adults learn. These are facts that you need to consider when delivering training: how to prime the brain to learn, time scales for learning periods, how the memory works and the different types of memory we use to learn. There is also a set of rules to help you apply this information to training courses. We then look at individual preferences in learning, how people prefer to process new information and how personality should be taken into account when delivering training.

Mind set

If the brain is 'warmed up' before a training module then the facts presented will be retained more efficiently. This warm-up session should take the form of a recap on existing knowledge with a section encouraging active learning. Active learning takes place when the participants are actively looking for ways to solve a problem and are encouraged to ask questions and contribute to the learning that is taking place. They should be continually encouraged to relate new information to what they already know. Clear goals should be set. These should be simply expressed, measurable, achievable, properly resourced and timed. They should be referred to throughout the learning process to remind the group what it is they are working to achieve.

If you have a group that seems sluggish, it is sometimes necessary to prime their brains to learn. You could do this by explaining that you are going to do some limbering up exercises for the brain and then present a set of conundrums of the 'two fathers and two sons shot three pheasants, each of them took home a pheasant, how could this be possible' nature. Alternatively, ask the group to play a memory game. There are many source books for this sort of brain exercise, among the best being *Psychological Games* by Nicola Alberto De Carlo (1984). I keep a large selection of loose sheets of puzzles, conundrums and quizzes that can be used on any course.

Having warmed their brains up, you now need to re-focus them on the task in hand. Ask them to write down anything that worries or interests them about what they are about to learn. Collect these on a flip chart, stick it up and refer back to it during the module.

Learning periods

Taking frequent, short breaks increases the ability to remember (the 'Zeigarnik Effect'). No session should last longer than 30 minutes maximum, and even though you may feel that the session is going really well, you should make sure that there are these frequent breaks engineered into the course. The breaks need to be up to 10 minutes long, but not much longer, and should involve a change in physical position (thank heavens for coffee machines). Over-teaching is a pointless exercise – trying to cram information into tired brains will result in loss of previously well understood facts.

Primacy and recency

The start and the end of a training module are the parts that will be best remembered. Essential information should be presented at the start of a module and recapped at the end with links to the forthcoming modules to encourage active learning. Putting vital information in the middle of a module with a weak or fact-free start and end is not the best way to anchor the important facts in the participants' minds.

Memory surge

A few minutes after being presented with new material, the memory seems to surge into action, recalling and organising more material than you would expect. It seems sensible to capitalise on this surge by setting tasks that utilise the new information (practice sessions, role plays, discussion groups) as quickly as possible after the information is first presented to the participants.

Outstanding elements (the 'Von Resdorff Effect')

Any information that is surprising or stands out from the rest of the information round it is likely to be remembered more clearly. When introducing a new set of facts, make the opening slide or statements vivid, use imaginative examples, make your language more exciting. This is why making excellent visual aids is such a help to learning, really important facts can be presented vividly with very little effort. (See Appendix D.)

Types of memory

Ultra short-term or sensory memory

This is the part of the memory where new input (from the eyes, ears or any other sense organ) is held while you select what you wish to consider and work with. It is very limited indeed – not just in time scales but in capacity. The ultra short-term memory is the gateway through which all information must pass before we can process it. If we try to pay attention to too many things at once then 'sensory overload' occurs and the brain rejects the input. Seven inputs at once is the limit for most people.

> Try this exercise next time you are with a group of friends. Ask them to listen carefully and then repeat back to you what you have said, word for word. Then give them a random list of five objects, for instance, 'dog, shoe, fish, umbrella, cake'. They should have no trouble with this, but if you continue with another list of seven objects, e.g. 'candle, computer, turtle, hairdresser, hand, book, telephone', you will find that they are beginning to muddle them up and forget individual items. If you then give them a list of about fourteen items, you will find that when you get past the tenth or eleventh, they will involuntarily laugh. This is because sensory overload has occurred and the idiocy of trying to remember all that information at once has struck them.

This overload effect does not apply only to the information you are presenting but also to the surroundings in which you are learning – background noise and movement, clutter and mess all work against successful input. To overcome the limitations of the ultra short-term memory you need to break new information into digestible chunks, making sure that each chunk has been clearly heard or seen before going on to react to that information and make sense of it.

The short-term memory

This is where you react to the new information, and this too can suffer from overload. To take information from the short-term to the working memory it is necessary to repeat the new information several times. Using visual aids, referring to manuals and putting vital information on a flip chart all help to repeat information in a varied way. If you have to give complicated strings of instructions (for example, when training people to use technical equipment or machinery) then break the information down, linking facts or commands together in logical groups.

The working memory

Until we have 'rehearsed' new information by repeating it to ourselves, compared it with existing information and judged the validity or usefulness of it, we have not fully encoded what we have heard or seen. This takes place within the working memory.

It is here that we make sense of what we are learning. People seem to go through a series of processes when they are encoding new information:

▌ First they react to what they have seen or heard, asking themselves questions like 'What is this about? What has this to do with me? Do I need to understand the words that I'm hearing, seeing or reading?'

▎ Then they make a judgement, 'Do I believe this? Does this seem reasonable?'

▎ Then they begin to compare, 'Does any of this sound familiar? Have I any past experience that will help me to understand?'

▎ Finally they begin to integrate new information with existing knowledge. They put it into their own words, they prioritise it and they relate it to their own tried and tested experience.

When all this has been done they put into practice what they have learned. They usually adapt and very often re-design the way they will use the information so that it conforms to their own patterns.

You will note that the working memory is continually shuttling between the new information and the information already held in the long-term memory. Take the example of your first driving lesson. The driving instructor starts by showing the main controls of the car. He points out the steering wheel, the clutch, the accelerator, the brake, the handbrake and the gear lever. Note that he is careful not to overload the short-term memory. The learner driver looks at each item, internally repeating the names of the things that seem unfamiliar. Probably passing through his mind is a set of memories of watching other people drive a car. Some of the new items are unfamiliar (probably the clutch, accelerator and foot brake) so he will want to put his feet on them, noting where the left and right feet are in relation to them and internally noting that accelerators make things go faster, brakes slow things down and the clutch is a bit of a mystery. A good driving instructor does not immediately go into the way to use each control, but allows the learner to become familiar and comfortable with the way they are arranged and even more importantly, encourages the learner to ask questions. Only when the basic facts have been assimilated and internalised is the learner ready to continue.

The long-term memory: semantic, episodic, spatial and visual memory

The long-term memory (which can hold information for decades) holds several different types of memories. Semantic memory holds new information that has been translated into our own internal codes. Episodic memory is where the memory of events is held – this can be very vivid but is influenced by our attitudes, expectations and preferences so is often not as accurate as we would like. Spatial memory is where positioning information is held and also includes visual pictures of what we have seen and remembered.

Hierarchy of memory

Visual memory Our visual memory is very strong – probably because the brain actually 'names' things before processing them visually. It is also the type of memory that is least likely to be distorted by internal processing. Harnessing the visual memory on training courses will bring tremendous benefits in terms of recall. The use of imagery – concrete images on slides and internal imagery by 'conjuring up a picture' can make the difference between only 20 per cent of a course's contents being retained and 50 per cent or more being integrated into the participant's existing knowledge base.

Aural memory Our memory for other people's words is not as reliable as many people think it is. Unless rhyme or rhythm is added to the meaning it is very unlikely that participants will remember what a trainer says by hearing it only once. Fortunately training courses are mainly to do with the interpretation and comprehension of the concepts behind the words a trainer uses, and not the literal repetition of the words. However there will be times when the exact wording of a command or sequence is critical – in this case make sure that there is written back-up of what needs to be remembered.

Episodic memory As I said before, our episodic memory is not as exact as it might be. We often distort what we think happened because of overlying attitudes and beliefs – for example, drivers after an accident quite often report behaviour on the part of others that simply did not happen; this is usually because an attempt is being made to explain away the randomness of accidents and partly because there is a need to present an exemplary front of guiltlessness. On training courses, particularly when gaining feedback on role plays, it is very useful to have input from the rest of the group who have not been actively involved in the role play.

Factual memory This is memory of things that people have not actually experienced, but is important basic information nonetheless – for example, the dates of important events in the past, critical examples of events that led up to a certain point, the names of people you have not actually met. We all have a need for this type of information but can only remember it by constant repetition. It helps if this kind of information can be integrated with working information that has already been internally processed.

Skills memory This is a set of complicated spatial, visual, motor, episodic, aural and semantic memories that are linked together to allow us to perform tasks like driving a car, operating a machine, typing, dancing, playing an instrument and so on. Skills memories can only develop with practice. The more practice, the better the skill. When you are skills training, the ratio between definition of the task and practice of the task should be 30:70.

Ordering, sorting and information integration

It is not enough merely to remember what has been presented on a course. For any meaningful change to take place the new information or skills have to be constructed into a meaningful whole. For example, the skills gained on a 'successful interviewing skills' course must be integrated with the communication skills, business awareness skills, judgements and practices that exist in business as a whole. For this to happen, information used to illustrate these basic skills should embody real information as far as possible. A framework for learning should be set up by using true case studies (names changed to protect the innocent), genuine situations, realistic role plays and basic ground rules. This infrastructure of reality underpins everything that happens on the course. After the course the real practice starts and the new skills will gradually be integrated with existing ones.

Applying these basic facts on a training course

The most important thing for a trainer to remember when delivering training is that most of the information you will be dealing with is already in your own long-term memory and is therefore easily called up when you need it. You will probably have forgotten how long it took you to remember, understand and integrate all these facts and skills in the first place. For most of the course participants this information is new, untested, untried and alien. In order to transfer these skills and packages of information to the people on the course the trainer must harness the way the memory actually works.

The pacing of a course is entirely within the trainer's control. It is up to the trainer to ensure that what has been presented has been adequately and accurately processed by the course participants. More information is not necessarily better – it is the way that the new information is integrated with the old that is of prime importance.

Without continual feedback from the group it is very difficult to know what has or has not been remembered and understood. Activities other than listening must be used to get your messages across and test whether they have been adequately processed.

A word of warning – self-evident truths

As trainers we constantly refresh our memories and integrate our information better by the very act of passing information on verbally and by example. This gives us the tremendous advantage of easily recalling and explaining our subjects and demonstrating our expertise, without having to go through the sometimes laborious loop of memory integration. This can give us a tendency to make assumptions about the base levels of knowledge in the participants – a very dangerous thing indeed. As an example, when I flew in a light aircraft for the first time, the pilot, who was not only experienced, but also knew the terrain we were flying over, kept pointing out things of interest as we passed over them. Several of these, like viaducts and historic buildings I could see clearly, but when we passed over a navigational beacon I had no idea what to look for – a bonfire on top of a hill perhaps? 'No, no, there!' he kept saying and flew round again to show me. I finally spotted a strange, geometric spider's web of wires and dishes in a field and then understood what he was talking about. He must have seen hundreds of navigational beacons and so assumed that everyone knew what they looked like, so had not bothered to give me the basic knowledge I needed to be able to recognise what I was looking for.

As trainers we must be sure that we make no assumptions about base knowledge. Check that what is self-evident to you is also self-evident to the participants.

Guidelines for effective learning

There are many things you can do as a trainer to ensure that the people on your courses learn effectively:

■ Warm up the participants' minds before you start a module. Recap on existing information, encourage active listening by asking questions and allowing them to question you. Set clear objectives and refer back to them.

- Watch out for sensory overload. Input information in a clear and ordered manner. Allow no distractions. Present information in meaningful chunks and not more than seven items at a time.

- Take frequent breaks, whether you feel you need them or not.

- Critical information should be presented at the start of a module and recapped at the end.

- Move information into the working memory by repeating critical points at least three times. Back up important aural information with reading matter or by encouraging the participants to visualise.

- Link all new information with existing information. Use anecdotes and analogies to illustrate your points.

- Allow the working memory time to encode the new information. Encourage discussion, debate and comment where people can use their own words.

- Use realistic role plays and case studies.

- When skills training allow 70 per cent of the available time for practice.

- Practice sessions should follow as soon as possible after the initial information has been relayed to the group.

- Expect people to react, judge, compare, integrate and finally adapt new knowledge and allow time for this.

- Visual memory is extremely strong and unlikely to be distorted. Use visual examples as much as possible.

- The final part of true learning will probably take place after the course. Set post-course exercises that will help this.

Individual preferences in learning

It is unlikely that any two people would set about learning in the same way. It is extremely unlikely that you will ever meet a group of people who are all comfortable with just one method of learning or processing information. Here we will look at the three areas of learning preferences.

Learning preferences

We each have personal preferences about how we like to take in information. Knowing in advance how people prefer to learn will allow you to tailor the course delivery method to suit the course participants. Over the years I have come to recognise that not only do individuals have learning preferences but so do companies: where an informal, participative approach would go down well for people from one company, people from another company may prefer a more structured and formal methodology.

Obviously you have learning preferences yourself. Ask yourself the following questions:

1   Do I like working alone?
2   Am I happiest working in a group?
3   Do I need to examine the evidence before I try anything new?
4   Do I hate general discussion?
5   Do I need to discuss things before I make up my mind?
6   Do I like role-play exercises?
7   Do I like being the centre of attention?
8   Do I need a manual to learn from?
9   Am I happiest working things out for myself?
10   Am I prepared to challenge the trainer if I feel that I need to?
11   Do I mind admitting that I do not know certain things?
12   Am I prepared to open up a discussion?
13   Do I prefer to wait until someone else has contributed before I speak up?
14   Do I like leading a group?

15 Do I prefer to be a group member?

16 Do I like to take detailed notes?

17 Am I prepared to do overnight work if necessary?

18 Do I mind being assessed by others?

19 Do I learn more quickly than most?

20 Do I learn more slowly then most?

21 Do I like to know the theory behind new concepts?

22 Am I the sort of person who likes to get on with things?

23 Am I cautious about trying out new skills?

24 Am I prepared to experiment?

25 Do I mind making mistakes?

Now ask the same questions of a colleague. You will almost certainly find that he or she has different answers to yours. It is obvious that someone who prefers to work alone, taking copious notes and who needs to examine the evidence before trying anything new has a different set of learning needs to someone who is happiest in a group, likes experimentation and adores being the centre of attention. Chapter 6 ('Training Techniques') looks into ways of coping with these differing learning needs.

Ideally it would be wonderful to know individual learning preferences well before the course so that if you had a particularly lively and outgoing group you could organise the course to cope with this. However, it is much more likely that you will have a mixture of learning preferences (and thinking styles, see next section) and so you should cater for all preferences by having a mixture of group activities, individual exercises, fact-based sessions, discussions, presentations, question and answer sessions, paper and pencil exercises, individual research or reading and role-play situations (where relevant).

Here is a summary of the preferences that you are likely to encounter on a training course. I have called them the 'get on with it', 'get it right', 'think about it' and 'make it work' styles. It is important to remember that no-one is totally one style, we are all a mixture and can use our less dominant preferences when we wish to.

Behaviour	Get On With It	Get It Right	Think About It	Make It Work
Speed of working	Likes to get on with things	Likes to take time	Likes to look at all sides of the picture	Likes to get things done, efficiently
Need for detail	Low	High	Low – prefers to discuss	Medium – if the details are useful
Importance of documentation	Low, prefers doing to reading	Very high, feels unsafe without it	Low – prefers to discuss	Medium – will use it if useful
Risk taking	Not worried	Very cautious	Needs discussion	Needs proof
Group activities	Likes them	Prefers to work alone	Likes them	Likes to lead
Attitude to feedback	Likes giving and receiving	Likes receiving, slow to give	Likes giving and receiving	Prefers factual feedback
Roles within the group	Leader, supporter, opponent	Outsider, supporter, opponent	Supporter, leader	Opponent, leader, outsider
Happiest when	Active, joining in, performing	Collecting data, checking, observing, evaluating	Discussing, putting things in perspective	Leading, challenging, evaluating
Unhappiest when	Being ignored, having to wait	Being hurried, being pushed	Being given point solutions	Wasting time or effort
Preferred interaction	Personal, disclosive	Impersonal, factual	Personal, logical, holistic	Impersonal, value for money

In a perfect world (from the trainer's viewpoint), everyone in the audience would have the same personality mix as ourselves – however, the world is not perfect and our audiences have their own funny little ways that are often in conflict with our own training styles if we rely too heavily on only one facet of our personality.

Here are some tips on how to keep each personality mix happy.

If you are heavily 'get on with it'

■ The 'get on with its' will love you.

■ The 'get it rights' will think you are going too fast, not giving them enough information or detail and may feel pressured. Slow down a little, make sure that you have comprehensive back-up material.

■ The 'think about its' will be well disposed towards you, but will feel that you may be focusing on spot solutions and not looking at the overall picture. Make sure that you are logical and show that you have thought about the consequences of what you are teaching.

■ The 'make it works' may well disbelieve you if you do not give enough evidence to prove what you are saying, and they will certainly check all your facts – so make sure that you have got them right.

If you are heavily 'get it right'

■ The 'get it rights' will listen carefully to you.

■ The 'get on with its' will become very bored if you present too many facts to them – they will want to know how it affects them. You may need to speed up a little for them. Try to show more animation.

■ The 'think about its' are on your side – so long as you don't go into too much detail and ignore the impact of what you are proposing on the whole business picture.

■ The 'make it works' will believe you, but will feel that you are wasting their time if you become too detailed and fail to show them how useful, cost- and time-effective and businesslike your information is.

If you are heavily 'think about it'

■ The 'think about its' will really enjoy your course.

■ The 'get on with its' will like what you are saying, but will want to know how it affects them personally, and would like you to go faster.

■ The 'get it rights' will like your pace, but will need more guidance and hard information.

■ The 'make it works' will think you are waffling if you do not stick to the business case.

If you are heavily 'make it work'

■ The 'make it works' will agree with you.

■ The 'get on with its' will like your pace, but feel that you are bullying them if you do not make them feel personally involved.

■ The 'get it rights' will like your approach but may need more detail.

■ The 'think about its' may feel that you are being too mechanistic unless you consider the impact of what you are saying on the people involved.

Preferred thinking styles

Apart from the influence that our preferred way of learning has on our response to new information, there is another very important individual factor that needs to be considered – which sensory system do people prefer to use when perceiving and making sense of new information? In the early 1970s, neuro-linguistic programming (NLP) was developed as a way of looking at how people process information, feelings, ideas and experiences. Some people are happiest when perceiving things through their eyes, making pictures in their heads: they are known as 'visuals'. Others respond better to auditory input – particularly the tone of voice and inflections used – and are most comfortable listening to and talking about the new information: they are known as 'aurals'. Others are more influenced by physical feelings like touch, movement, smell and taste: 'kinaesics'. Others are most interested in the words themselves, conducting internal conversations with the little voice inside their heads: 'digitals'. In any course you are bound to have a mixture of 'visual', 'auditory', 'kinaesic' and 'digital' thinkers. A trainer who makes sure that all the bases are covered will have a much greater chance of success. Here is a table summarising the best learning environment for each style.

Influence	Visuals	Aurals	Kinaesics	Digitals
Environment	Likes orderliness, attractive surroundings	Distracted by external noise	Needs room to move about	Dislikes interruptions
Documentation and visual aids	Likes pictures, diagrams, colours	Dislikes long descriptions, not interested in pictures	Not particularly interested in reading	Likes to translate to internal dialogue
Data collection	Takes notes, mind maps, plans or flow charts	Needs verbal repetition, from self and others	Remembers activity	Internalises, may feed it back later
Stress or boredom	Stares around	Talks it out	Gestures, fidgets	Closes up

Preferred focus and personal priorities

Think about the following statements:

> 1 At work my primary task is to get the job done.
> 2 I like to get to know someone before I work with them.
> 3 Making good relationships with my colleagues is an integral part of my job.
> 4 I judge people by how they behave with me.
> 5 I judge people by how they perform the tasks they need to do.
> 6 I am comfortable revealing information about my personal life.
> 7 I am uncomfortable revealing information about my personal life.
> 8 I like to stick to the point.

If you feel that numbers 1, 5, 7 and 8 are very true about yourself, then when you train you may feel that there is no particular need to get to know the course participants personally and that your best training courses are the ones that get the information across efficiently and without personalising the learning process. If, on the other hand you feel that 2, 3, 4 and 6 are more true of yourself, then you probably feel that a personal relationship with the participants is a vital part of the course and that learning cannot take place without this.

These are obviously two very different approaches to training, and so long as the group that you are training feel the same way as you then all should be well. However, what do you do if you find that there are people on the course who do not feel the same way as you? The answer is that the trainer has to adapt, and it is easier to do this if you have some idea of what to expect. If you do not know the people who will be coming onto the course, then you should try to meet them before the course actually starts

– or at the very least try to evaluate their focus and priorities during the start-up phase of training. It is also worth asking for a 'thumbnail sketch' of each participant from the commissioning manager – but remember that this will be a subjective evaluation.

In brief

■ No training course can succeed if the participants remember nothing of it, or cannot make sense of the information presented to them. Trying to pack as much information as possible into a training course is counter-productive, it simply will not be processed if you overload the memory.

■ Try to use as many and varied methodologies as you can to get your point across. Make sure that you organise activities that will allow the information to be effectively internalised – it is not enough just to present the facts, you need to use role play, exercises and activities to integrate what has been learned.

■ Although you may deliver the same material time after time, each course must be adjusted to the different learning preferences, thinking styles and priorities that will inevitably characterise each different group of participants.

One final word

> 'Memories may escape the action of the will, may sleep a long time, but when stirred by the right influence, though that influence be but as light as a shadow, they flash into life with everything in place.'
>
> John Muir.

A good trainer should be that influence.

6

Training Techniques

Bearing in mind all that has been said about adapting our delivery methods to suit the personal needs of the participants, now is the time to look at some of the training techniques available to us.

The training techniques we shall be considering here are:

■ the lecture
■ the demonstration
■ technical training
■ interactive training
 ☐ discussion and group learning
 ☐ the role play
■ learning through questions
■ adventure learning
■ individual learning
■ feedback.

Each technique has its place in a training course – it is up to the trainer to choose the most appropriate one.

Lectures and demonstrations

> *Lec.ture* n : a discourse given before an audience or class esp. for instruction.

The lecture is the most formal of all training methods. It requires the audience to sit still and listen, usually leaving questions until the lecturer has finished. In its way it is rather like a formal presentation, stating the facts clearly and in a logical order, illustrating them with examples and possibly visual aids, finally summarising and opening the subject to the audience. It has its place in training but is frequently over-used, particularly by trainers who are worried by the thought of an unruly audience or the dangers of uncontrolled interaction.

The mini-lecture is most useful when you need to introduce new information to a group quickly, but it should always be followed by a period of practice, discussion, individual or group learning. This will consolidate the information and prove that the group have learned and can use the new information for themselves.

Here are the rules:

- no longer than 20 minutes
- careful structure:
    - tell them what it is about
    - tell them about it, illustrated with 'for instances'
    - summarise the main points
- encourage questions afterwards
- no more than seven main points
- no more than seven slides
- back it up with a handout
- reinforce the information by linking it up to other modules in the rest of the course.

The lecture is enjoyed most by participants who are 'information collectors', who like to think things through before committing themselves and who are not irritated by having to sit still with no interaction. Lecture-based learning is often an efficient way of getting information across to large numbers of people quickly, but will almost always need a backup period of activity or personal involvement to drive the information home.

The demonstration

> *Dem.on.strate* vt 1: to show clearly 2a: to prove or make clear by reasoning or evidence b: to illustrate or explain esp. with many examples 3: to show or prove the value or efficiency of to a prospective buyer 4: a show of armed force.

The demonstration is particularly useful when showing a group or a person how to use new technology. A good demonstration should serve these purposes:

- to show visually how things link together
- to simplify what may at first seem complicated
- to show cause and effect
- to explain what sequence of events are needed to use the product
- to allay any doubts or worries about the product
- to encourage the group/person to use the product
- to discover the user's detailed needs
- to show the most efficient way of using the product
- to show the capabilities of the product.

There are basically three types of demonstration:

- The performance demo, or 'watch my magic fingers'
- The teaching demo
- The interactive demo.

The performance demo

This is where the accomplished operator sits down at the technology and gives a virtuoso rendition of that old favourite – 'I'm doing this so fast that no one can tell what I'm up to but my goodness – the results look impressive!' There is no place for this on a training course. It scares the daylights out of the inexperienced, it makes the kit look difficult to use and it teaches absolutely nothing.

The teaching demo

This is an excellent training tool as long as these simple rules are followed:

> ▮ Introduce the demo very clearly. 'What I am going to show you is… this will be useful to you when you need to… page ** in the manual covers these points.'
> ▮ Do not attempt to do too much.
> ▮ Link the new skills to existing skills. 'Now that we know how to log into the system we are going to create a file to work in…'
> ▮ Say what you are going to do.
> ▮ Do it slowly.
> ▮ Recap on what you did.
> ▮ Do not take any short-cuts.
> ▮ Explain all technical terms in plain English.
> ▮ Make sure you can be seen and heard.
> ▮ Do not hurry, but do not take too long, the trainees will want to try it for themselves.

As with the lecture, this methodology is appreciated by people who like to watch and observe before trying. Participants who like to join in and try for themselves will be much happier with an interactive demonstration.

The interactive demo

This is an excellent tool both to introduce new skills and to help cure any faulty skills. The secret of a good interactive demo is to allow the trainee to do most of the talking, only joining in to explain or set tasks. This is how to do it:

- Find out from the participant what he or she needs to learn.

- Find out how much he or she already knows (you can do this by asking them to show you a particular technique).

- Set a new task, explaining clearly why they need to know this and what the outcome will be.

- If there is no way that the participant can work the new task out, then demonstrate slowly, using the teaching demo techniques.

- Ask the participant to try it – twice at least.

- Get them to explain what they did.

- If they make a persistent mistake, show them again using positive reinforcement (pointing out what they are doing right and encouraging them to change what they are doing wrong).

- Move on to the next task, linking it to the one just learned.

- Keep an eye on the time – don't let them work for more than 20 minutes without a break.

- At the end of the session, ask them to tell you what they have learned.

- Praise when they do well – but be specific.

Interactive demonstrations will keep most people happy. They allow the 'get on with its' to get on with it, the 'get it rights' to reassure themselves that they have got it right, the 'think about its' to discuss and think about it, and the 'make it works' to make it work efficiently. The only factor that needs to concern the trainer is speed: do not expect everyone to work at the same pace, you will need to have extra exercises to keep the ones who like to work fast busy while they wait for the more cautious to catch up.

Technical training

Tech.ni.cal adj a: having special and usu. practical
knowledge esp. of a mechanical or scientific subject.
b: of or relating to a particular subject esp: a practical
subject organised on scientific principles.

Technical training presents several challenges with which
less specialised training is unconcerned:

▌ Technical language (jargon): in most training,
jargon should be assiduously avoided. However,
in technical training the users must become
familiar with the technical terms needed in order
to ask other specialists for advice, to report faults
to manufacturers and, indeed, to talk to other
specialists in the language that they all understand.

▌ Fairly rigid procedures: there are always several
ways of using technology, but some are more
efficient than others and these are the ones that
need teaching.

▌ Fear: new users of technology are terrified of it –
they are afraid of failing, afraid of looking stupid,
afraid of breaking the equipment, afraid that they
will lose their old skills…

▌ Necessary background knowledge: it is important
for the user to understand the basic principles
behind the technology, or the learning is only
'parrot fashion' and useless in a situation where a
mistake needs rectifying.

▌ Safety and legal procedures: there is often a need
to know and perform several procedures that are
time-consuming and not particularly interesting
– backing up computer disks, for instance.
Training people to realise the importance of these
is difficult since most of us would prefer not to
undertake the extra effort they require.

Overcoming the problems of technical training
Sound knowledge on the part of the trainer

You must know your stuff, and understand it fully. Preparation is the key here. When learning new technologies yourself, keep a notebook by you and note down which things you found the hardest. These are the very things your trainees will find difficult, and where you will need to spend extra time on the course.

Technical language

A Glossary of Terms is essential. Put the main technical terms up on a large flip chart, with their meanings. Run a little quiz at the beginning of each session.

Whenever you need to introduce a new term, give a full explanation of it and reinforce this several times. It is amazing how many technical terms we use as if they were familiar to the entire world.

Necessary background knowledge

How is it plugged in? How do you switch it on? What connects to what? What if there is a power failure? What can I touch? How do you switch it off? How do you disconnect it? Is it breakable? How do I keep it clean? Where is the information stored? If I do not type it in, where has it come from? Is there anything I have to do each day – at the beginning? At the end? Who can I contact when it goes wrong or when I go wrong? Where is the information stored? Is there a manual? How do I use it? Think through all the basic questions that you asked when you were first faced with this new technology and make sure you have all the answers. Make a list of all the basic facts that the users must know and all the facts that would make the users feel more comfortable. Put it in the manual, pin it on the wall, tell them about it!

Ignorance is *not* bliss. Ignorance is frightening – particularly to a new user. Anything you can do to reassure them will make your job as a trainer easier. The pure theory behind technology should mainly be left alone – after all, we do not need to know about the physics of water pressure and rotation to be able to use a washing machine. But we do need to know where to switch it off should a flood occur!

Fear

We know it is robust. The manufacturer knows it is robust, the guy who mends it knows it is robust, the experienced user knows it is robust and the salesman knows it is robust. The new user thinks it is made of Meissen porcelain and spun glass and is bound to break, catch fire, make a horrible noise, electrocute you, emit deadly rays, make the telephones faulty, lose the data, go wrong, make him or her look silly, make him or her redundant…

As trainers, the first barrier we have to break is the fear barrier. So reassure first, never stress the aspects that might cause difficulty – 'on our machines… never!'. Guide the new user from safety to safety, stressing the positives. If you come to a technically complex part of the training, do not say 'now this bit is really difficult'. Rather, say something like: 'this is important, so we will go through it carefully.'

And if by any awful chance you do have a breakdown (technical, not nervous) during a course, use it as a positive chance to show retrieval procedures, as an example of the bomb-proof qualities of the software/hardware/service contract/help line/back-up procedures.

There is another aspect of the unease that new users feel – they are all familiar with the technology that they use every day, and in several areas they are experts in subjects that you as a trainer probably know nothing about. And yet here they are, having to go back to school to learn new skills, a new language and a new environment. It is not surprising that they are wary of asking questions or asking for clarification. Try as often as you can to get them to question you, to ask you to explain again. And try to remain patient when you have to explain things for the 14th time – what is obvious to you may be a mystery to them!

Rigid procedures/safety and legal considerations

You cannot get away from them so make them as clear and simple as possible. Checklists and short reference cards help here, as do manuals and mnemonics. Examples are:

S.P. L.U.R.G.E –

Switch it on

Power it up

Log yourself in

Update the user list

Read the new mail

Get the new info in

End the session.

Technical training by its very nature tends to be less interactive than skills training. This sometimes leads to a rather static and potentially rigid course, where the main interaction comes in the form of question and answer sessions. Efficiency becomes the watchword without consideration of enjoyment. It is not in everyone's nature to find the collection of useful data a delightful pastime. The more energetic 'get on with its' may feel that their need for recognition and rapport is being neglected, while the thoughtful 'think about its' will miss the opportunity for discussion. You need to judge when the course needs livening up and arrange team quizzes and discussions about how the participants will actually use their new skills back at the workplace. Always remember – technical courses need just as careful a start-up session as any other course.

Thinking point

It is often on technical courses that 'over-teaching' occurs. There is considerable pressure on the trainer to cover all the contents of the often bulky user manuals. This is probably impossible, given that these were written by expert technical writers whose life's work is producing manuals that cover every option. Unless you have designed the course yourself, it is vital to go through the manuals and decide what must be known, what is useful to know, what is nice to know and what is possible to discover afterwards, once the basic skills have been achieved. Once you have prioritised the areas you are going to cover, think about the realistic capacity of the human brain and memory and act accordingly.

Interactive training

Inter.act vi: to act upon one another

in.ter.ac.tion n: mutual or reciprocal action or influence.

This is where you hang up your traditional teacher's hat and become a facilitator. To facilitate is to do something that makes an action, a happening or a change possible. Here you use your skills to help the trainees discover. This is a particularly effective methodology for participants who need to join in, experiment, verbalise new ideas and take chances. Here you are not the wisdom or information-giver, you are merely the guide and helper. In fact you must keep a tight rein on your subject-expertise.

Interactive training allows the participants to learn for themselves – to discover, to practise, to discuss, to learn through mistakes, to develop, to explore, to refine. You as trainer take a back seat role, not telling or demonstrating, merely acting as a steersman to the learning process. The participants are the captains and sail their own ships. You point out where the rocks and whirlpools are, but if the captains still decide to take that route, they will learn from their mistakes – and most of all from their successes.

Your tasks as an interactive trainer are just as onerous as when you are a platform trainer – at times more so. You have to make sure that everyone takes part, that they understand what they are doing, and that they keep to the subject. You also have to look after the organisation of the training room, time scales and break times. It is hard, but it is worth it.

Discussion and group learning

Dis.cus.sion n: consideration of a question in open and usually informal debate.

Here the trainer kicks the discussion off, and keeps it going, without adding his or her information and expertise until everyone has had their say. The benefits of discussion are that each trainee brings his or her experience to the problem at hand. The trainer also acts as the organiser. Here are the tasks that the trainer should perform during a discussion:

- Set the topic: make sure that this is clearly expressed and displayed.
- Keep the trainees to the subject: a gentle reminder of where they are in the discussion helps when they get sidetracked.
- Make sure everyone has a chance to speak: the trainer needs to arbitrate if a particular trainee – and there is always one! – starts to hog the floor.
- Encourage the quiet ones to speak.
- Summarise what has been said and either take notes or write the findings up on a flip chart.
- Keep to time.
- Ask for input from the 'outsiders' in the group.

Most participants enjoy discussion as a learning method, particularly if the discussion sessions help to relate the skills and information gained on the course to the outside world. The 'get it rights', though, may be slow to join in because they are wary of committing themselves without hearing what others have to say. These are the ones that the trainer needs to encourage to speak when everyone else has had their say.

Group learning is often similar to discussion as a training technique. Here the trainees run the session for themselves with the trainer facilitating and organising, but not chairing. The trainer may offer help by giving advice, but must never solve the group's problems for them. The group works as a whole with each member helping or being helped by the group.

These are the requirements for a group to learn effectively together:

- The group must be small enough to give everyone the courage and the opportunity to talk (4–6), yet large enough to ensure that enough opinions, experience and knowledge are shared.
- All group members should be treated as equal.
- Different group members should chair the discussions/activities in turn.
- The group members must be prepared for the exercise – they must be aware that they are in charge of this type of learning, and that you as a trainer are not in command.
- The group should test itself on the learning achieved – see page 101 'Learning through questions'.

Group learning is an effective way of solving real problems. For example, on project management courses I always include a group-learning session where the participants have to solve a genuine problem that has occurred in one of their company's projects. They know, far better than any trainer, the ins and outs of projects in their company, and can pool their knowledge to real effect.

The role play

There comes a time on every training course when you and the participants need to see whether the things they have learned can be put into practice. This is particularly true when you have been covering behavioural skills – training skills, demonstration skills, management skills, interviewing skills and so on.

The role play allows you to do this for these reasons:

> ■ It mimics a 'real' situation and allows the participants to practise without too much stress.
>
> ■ It allows the participants to try out alternative behaviours.
>
> ■ It provides an opportunity for feedback on how they performed, both from the trainer and the rest of the course.
>
> ■ If video is used, the participants learn an enormous amount from self-criticism – particularly on body language and communication.

However, since the training course is not the actual business situation in which the trainees will be using their newly acquired skills, the role play requires a certain 'suspension of disbelief'. This is why any role play must be carefully researched.

Many people really dislike the idea of the role play – they see it as play acting, larking about, unreal, time consuming, an opportunity for settling old scores and so on. This is why all role plays must be set up carefully and should not contain any elements that are likely to lead to embarrassment or outright failure.

It is necessary to point out that when role-playing you are being yourself, not an actor. For example, if you are running a role play on an interviewing skills course, the participants playing the interviewers are definitely testing out their personal skills, but the participants playing the interviewees may feel that they are having to be something they are not. This is not true. Practically everyone who works for a company will have been through the interview process and so can identify with what is going on and behave realistically in the role play. Added to this, the very act of putting yourself into the other person's shoes very often leads to valuable insights into how you interact with other people.

Here are the rules for setting up and running a successful role play:

▋ Always try to work with real case studies. If you do not know enough about the company you are training, ask the participants to develop a role-play situation from their own experience. For example, role play an internal training session. They will know who they will be training, in what skills and under what circumstances. Both you and they will know which skills they need to practise, and what they want to look out for and receive feedback on.

▋ Write these things on a flip chart and display them:

The objectives for the role play
To examine how to handle a slow learner.

The characters in the role play
The trainer; Felicity Ffarnes-Barnes, the trainee.

The scenario
At Felicity's desk in a crowded office.

The timings
15 minutes role play, 15 minutes feedback.

Equipment needed
    Electronic mail terminal
    User list
    Outgoing mail
    Printer
    Notepad
    Manual
    Reminder sheet

The plot

Felicity has tremendous difficulty in using her terminal: she persistently loses her text and mis-files the incoming mail. The trainer needs to teach her to use a consistent set of commands and to be systematic in how she stores her files.

The tasks

Check log-on procedures, set up good user habits, teach consistency.

Feedback looked for

Speed of training

Clarity of explanations

Interpersonal skills.

- Give the participants time to prepare – at least a quarter of an hour.

- Set up the camera.

- Start the role play. Remember to switch the camera on, but it is better then to leave the camera recording and sit with the rest of the trainees during the role play – the camera seems more intrusive if there is an operator standing by it.

- The rest of the group should be making notes during the role play so that feedback will be clear.

- When time is up, switch the camera off, rewind and seat the group so that they can see the screen clearly. The participants should have the best view.

- Remind the group of the Feedback rules (see page 106).

Ideas for role plays

The reverse role play. Here the participants have to do everything wrong! It is surprising how much you can learn by watching yourself deliberately making mistakes. This is a role-play technique I often use on presentation courses where the participants can obviously present well and structure their presentations efficiently, but are being tremendously formal and distant in their approach. Asking them to do a reverse role play (with adequate time to prepare) loosens them up, lightens the mood of the course and gives them licence to make others laugh.

The 'helicopter view' role play. Here there are three participants involved, two role-playing and the third ready to step in and take over after a defined period of time. The ex-role player then has the chance to sit back and re-strategise, while the role play continues.

All role play exercises must be followed by a feedback session, which allows the participants and audience to analyse what they did well and what they want to change (see page 105).

Learning through questions

> *Ques.tion* n: an interrogative expression often used to test knowledge.

The technique of learning through questions is probably one of the oldest training techniques in existence – the Ancient Greeks used it, as did the Egyptians and the Chinese. It is so successful because it encourages the students to choose what they really want to know and then discover for themselves what the answers are. There is no redundancy and no waste.

This is how it works:

> For each area of learning, the trainees select seven questions to which they need answers. They then have several choices of how to find out these answers:
>
> ▮ Find an expert and ask.
> ▮ Try out for themselves.
> ▮ Find a reference book.
> ▮ Watch someone else doing it.
> ▮ Find cross-references and connections with knowledge already acquired.

The important thing is that the impetus for learning comes entirely from the trainee, without any pressure from outside. This is called 'learning through insight'.

The role of the trainer in this technique is to act as a guru, becoming a source of information, reference material and kit! The trainer does not offer unwanted or unrequested information but sticks entirely to the topics brought up by the trainee.

This technique works well with follow-up courses, where the participant needs to refine the knowledge or skill gained on the primary course.

The quiz and test

This is a splendid way of both checking learning and reinforcing new skills. During the course of each training module, the trainees are asked to write down questions about the information covered. At the end of the morning or afternoon they divide up into teams and ask each other their questions. The advantage of allowing the trainees to select the questions is that they 'own' the information, they focus on the parts that they have either understood or misunderstood, not on what the trainer assumes they will understand or misunderstand. And last, but not least, they make up much tougher questions than most trainers!

Adventure learning

Outward Bound courses, physical skills training and some management training and team-building activities all come under the heading of adventure learning. Here the venue for the course is away from the business place and the skills being taught or activities being facilitated are not as overtly business-based as more formal internal courses.

In adventure learning the participants are encouraged to develop skills that highlight the way they work with other team members, and learn new skills while examining their attitudes to change, risk taking, leadership and so on. Some adventure learning courses are used as motivational events, rewards or conference activities. Most are highly enjoyable. However, many adventure learning courses may involve a certain amount of perceived physical risk or discomfort and present problems that the trainer based in the training room does not generally encounter.

How to run adventure-learning sessions

I interviewed Pete Thorn, a professional flying instructor who has many years experience of training people for their Private Pilot's Licence. Here is what he said:

You cannot train people who are being forced to do things they hate. If people are under duress they are not receptive to learning. They will put up all kinds of rationalisations and barriers to put off the evil hour when they have to start, and be positively looking for reasons *not* to do it if pushed. Make sure that they are committed to what they are being asked to do. There is a difference between understandable nervousness about a new environment or challenge and a genuine unwillingness to be in the situation in the first place.

Set really clear expectations. Adventure learning is not surprise learning. The goals and objectives for each session must be clearly defined. People who feel at risk will be looking for dragons around every corner, so they must know what is going to happen to them.

Encourage a dialogue. Participants should feel comfortable expressing misgivings, asking for more explanations and feeding back difficulties and worries. You should create this rapport from the moment the course starts.

Get them into the activities as soon as possible. This is not a theoretical experience – the people being trained need to experience what it is they are trying to learn. In the case of people learning to fly, parachute, climb rocks or whatever, take them up as soon as you have briefly covered any basic safety or legal matters and let them safely experience what they are starting to learn. Let them hold the controls, let them practise soft landings, practise climbing safe slopes. Get them into the activity and let them gain a sense of achievement as soon as possible.

Give them as much control as possible over what they are doing. Information is power. Ignorance is fear. Show them the safeguards and explain as much as necessary about what is happening and what is going to happen. Once they feel in control they will begin to build on their successes.

Foster success and not failure. Pay as much attention to the things that they do well as you do to correcting poor habits. Unless there is a rigid set of procedures or methods that *must* be followed, let the individual participants do things in their own style. You can always refine their performance later when they are comfortable with their new skills.

It goes without saying that unqualified or relatively inexperienced trainers should not attempt to run courses that involve genuine danger. The participants' first and foremost need is to be safe.

Individual learning

If individual learning works, who needs trainers? Most courses involve a certain amount of individual learning, whether it is looking at the manual, revising written material or reading background material. Evening work on residential or long courses might involve individual preparation for the following day, so what has the trainer to do with this, since he or she will probably be having a well deserved rest while the individual learning takes place? Well, unless the participants have second sight, they need to know what they are being asked to do. They need to have the task ahead of them set out clearly and logically. They need to know the following things:

▪ the objectives for the individual work
▪ the timescales involved
▪ the materials they will need

- the standards to which they will be working
- whether help is available to them
- what they will be asked to do after they have finished.

An instruction like 'look through the manual tonight' is simply not enough. It leaves the participant with no focus, and will lead to poor learning. Much better is an instruction like: 'Take half an hour to look through the manual, paying particular attention to the following sections: 2a, "Defining Project Statements"; 3c, "Project Management Tools" and 6b, "Risk Analysis in Short-term Projects". Tomorrow we will be working on the information contained in these sections. The exercises at the end of these sections contain three crucial questions. You will need to answer these by tomorrow.' This sets a goal to be achieved.

In all the years I have been training I have noticed that poor tasking for individual learning inevitably leads to the participants, rather shamefacedly, admitting the next day 'I didn't do the evening work'. By contrast, in my experience, carefully tasked evening work has always been done.

A word of warning

Through circumstances beyond anyone's control, sometimes it becomes impossible for the participant to fulfil the individual tasks set. If this is so, you may need to allow time on the course for these tasks to be done. In any event, if the evening or individual task is essential to a particular module on the course, you must allow time just before the module for the participants to recap or revise what they did.

Feedback

I have left feedback as a training technique until last since feedback of some sort or another should be used throughout the course, no matter what delivery technique you are using. Feedback works both ways. On the one hand it allows the trainer and other participants to tell the participants how they are doing. On the other hand it allows the participants to tell the trainer and the other participants how they feel they are doing. This is particularly important on personal skills courses where individual behaviours are under examination.

I have often been told by participants that the personal feedback sessions were one of the most important parts of a course because these sessions focused entirely on actual behaviours in role plays and exercises that the participant had not initially thought important and that could be changed to more appropriate ones. Feedback should concentrate on what people actually did and said rather than focus on personal traits. For example: 'Goodness, you are clumsy' is not constructive feedback, whereas 'When you tripped over the cables and knocked the projector over, you gave the impression of losing control' is more constructive.

In order to give effective feedback it is important to structure the sessions carefully.

Feedback rules

- Focus feedback on the behaviours rather than personalities.
- Focus feedback on observations rather than opinions.
- Focus feedback on descriptions rather than judgements.
- Be specific not general.
- Share ideas – do not give advice.
- Feed back on things that it is possible to change.
- Be sensitive of how the feedback is received.
- Start each feedback session with a positive comment, and encourage participants to do the same when feeding back their own feelings about their performance.

Giving feedback

When making a critique of a participant's performance, phrases such as these seem to work most effectively:

- 'What did you like about your performance?'
- 'What would you change?'
- 'What do the rest of you think?'
- 'I thought you did - - - really well.'
- 'Because - - - '
- 'Maybe you could try - - - next time.'
- 'What have you learned from this?' (Each participant should make their own list.)
- 'What will you do next time?' (Each participant should make their own list.)

Effective feedback really helps the participant to learn. Ineffective or careless feedback can do great harm and leave the participant feeling resentful and a failure. Always stress that it is up to the participant to decide what to change, and that feedback is there to help, not hinder.

In brief

- We have a multitude of training methods to choose from. Using varied approaches to learning brings variety and excitement to a course.

- The more formal methodologies (the lecture and formal demonstration) have a pattern to them which makes them easier to schedule and control. However, too great a reliance on these methods can ignore the needs of the extrovert participants in the group.

- The interactive methodologies need to be planned carefully to give the best results. People undoubtedly internalise information and integrate skills effectively by using these techniques, but unless these are systematically planned and tasked they can become too undefined to have real outcomes.

▌ Throughout all courses, carefully directed feedback is invaluable and will give clear pointers to participants about the success of their skills and behaviours.

▌ It is up to the trainer to choose the method that best fits not only the material being presented but also the participants involved in the course.

I shall leave the last word to Ralph Waldo Emerson:

> 'There is always a best way of doing everything, even if it be to boil an egg.'

7

Crisis in the Training Room

When I first started training, one of my major worries was that things might go wrong on the course and that I would lose control. I remember back at school we had a maths teacher who, although brilliant at the subject, had very poor control over her classes. As a result we made her life a misery, pushing the boundaries of bad behaviour back until she finally snapped and fled the classroom – and this was at an all-girls school! I was convinced that this might happen to me. In fact I need have had no such worries – it is very rare indeed for a group of adult participants to rise up and terrorise the trainer, and most of the potential disasters that occur on training courses are due to outside factors or poor planning and not rowdiness on the part of the participants.

This chapter starts with general crisis management and then covers some of the problems that might occur on a course, with ways of resolving them. The second half of the chapter covers negative behaviours on the part of participants that need to be changed in order for individual and group learning to take place.

Before you start worrying that these behaviours or crises will occur on every course, think back to all the courses you have attended. Most of them will have passed without incident and that is what it is usually like in the real world. However, forewarned is forearmed, so here we go.

In the 20 or so years I have been training all of these have happened to me:

- logistics problems
    - ☐ no trainees (poor course joining instructions)
    - ☐ course (waiting) in Belgium, trainer in Oxfordshire (my fault)
    - ☐ no guest speakers (conflicting appointments)
    - ☐ no equipment (van broke down)
    - ☐ no software (disks corrupted)
    - ☐ no manuals (late delivery)
- venue problems
    - ☐ no training room (double booking by hotel)
    - ☐ no accommodation for a residential course (organiser forgot to book)
    - ☐ no electricity (power cut)
    - ☐ no food (caterer did not arrive)
    - ☐ a flood (burst water tank)
    - ☐ the training room caught fire (hotel kitchen next door)
    - ☐ food poisoning affecting the whole course, including me! (seafood)
- participant problems
    - ☐ three trainees so drunk they did not make sense (alcoholics)
    - ☐ a physical fight (same alcoholics)
    - ☐ the police arrived (practical joke on the part of a participant)
    - ☐ the employing company went bankrupt during the course (recession)
    - ☐ two participants were made redundant during the course (recession)
- accidents and acts of God
    - ☐ I lost my voice (non-infectious hoarseness)

☐ an earthquake (act of God)

☐ a plague of greenfly (act of gardener)

☐ I fell in love on a course, and, Dear Reader, I married him.

Well – delivery vans break down, power supplies fail, nature cannot be controlled, course administrators can make mistakes, people are only human and if there's a spanner about, it often finds its way into the works!

How to cope with a crisis

These are the key things to remember:

Do not pretend it has not happened. This is the first and most important rule. Problems must be nipped in the bud or they will link together and grow worse. If problems arrive you need to investigate them as soon as possible. For example, I was once delivering training in a newly built training suite in an hotel which was being generally upgraded. Half an hour into the course workmen started drilling and hammering in the corridor outside the training room. The course participants were amused – they were used to this hotel, and made comments like 'It's always like this', and 'There they go again.' It would have been easy to just put up with it rather than make a fuss, but the noise was seriously interrupting the course. I called a short break, went to see the conference manager, and it was fixed without any fuss – and what is more we had better service from the hotel on that course than the participants expected.

Define the exact problem. Is it an irritation? Is it health-threatening? Did you specify exactly what you wanted from the venue? Who is responsible for fixing the problem? Is it part of a bigger problem? Is there anything that *can* be done? Before you start to fix things or complain you need to have as many facts as possible.

Do not panic: you will gain 'brownie points' for staying calm. It is nerve-racking at the start of a course, when you do not know the participants particularly well, they do not know each other very well and you may be in an unfamiliar environment, to have serious problems occurring. Take a deep breath and calm down. If you can solve the problem the participants will respect you and your authority for the rest of the course will be intact.

Keep careful records, do not exaggerate, stick to the facts. Do not trust hearsay, find out for yourself. Try always to get corroborative evidence or another witness. If outside circumstances have forced you to cancel a course then your company may well be entitled to compensation.

Let the course participants know what is happening. Leaving the participants in the dark is very unwise. If you have to call a break to sort out problems, be sure that you have activities available that can fill in the time while you are fixing things. Discussion exercises, extra reading (a chance to become familiar with the course materials), individual work and preparation for individual presentations can all fill in time – so long as the participants know what the problem was that caused the interruption to the course, and that you are fixing it, then they will be understanding.

Involve the participants (as far as possible) in helping to solve the problem. These are adults you are training – they may well have skills, contacts and influence that you do not possess.

If the circumstances warrant it, do not be afraid to cancel the course. There are times when nothing can be done except cancel the course. When the hotel caught fire during a presentation course I was delivering, for instance, the disruption was so severe, the smoke so thick, and all of us so alarmed that we simply could not continue. If the crisis in any way endangers the health or safety of the participants, you must cancel the course. I know that this may need sanction from a more senior manager, but the trainer is the captain of the course ship, so participants and children first; trainers last.

Natural disasters apart, most course breakdowns are the result of poor communication. This may be the fault of the trainer, the course administrator, the manager, the training centre or the delivery man, but not usually the participants.

Check, check and check again that everyone involved with the smooth running and logistics of the course knows what is expected of them.

Types of crisis

Course crises generally come under one of four headings: logistics crises, venue crises, participant crises, and accidents and acts of God.

Logistics crises

These are the most common problems, with suggested solutions:

No trainees. Find out why. If they can get there in a reasonable timescale, start the course with meticulous care. Be aware that if they are so late that the course will be seriously affected (guest speakers becoming unavailable, rooms not available for extra hours, no time for all the exercises, etc), it may well be better for all to try to reschedule the course and set another date. If by any awful mishap it is your fault or your team's fault that the trainers have been sent to the wrong place or given the wrong dates, you will have to do a serious damage limitation exercise (possibly offering an alternative course for free).

No guest speakers. Have a fill-in session prepared and see if you can re-schedule the guest speaker. I always make sure that I have the guest speaker's handouts with me on the course, so that I can stand in for the guest speaker if possible. Give the absentee speaker hell when you see them – he or she should be responsible for finding a replacement, not you.

No kit (hardware or software). This is a particularly nasty glitch when you are dealing with material that relies on computers or other machinery. Re-organise the course so that the theoretical learning that does not require the kit comes first; meanwhile organise the kit to appear at lunchtime. Set it up during the lunch break.

No manuals. Photocopy the first few pages of your manual during the first break. Organise the delivery of the missing manuals for lunchtime. Introduce the 'how to use the manual' session then.

Venue crises

These are the most common problems, with suggested courses of action:

No training room, no accommodation. Find out why. If it is the fault of the venue its management should be pushed to fix it if no training room or accommodation is available. This again may lead to course cancellation. Write an apology afterwards.

No power (heat, air conditioning, light etc). This is not your fault, and the course participants will understand. While the power is being put back on, organise a question and answer session or have a 'naming of parts' session. If there is no light, take a break. If the power loss is likely to be a long one, set private work or revision and hope that there is somewhere with light available. If not, stop.

No food. Go out to the nearest pub. Keep the drinking teetotal. Make sure that they get back on time.

Food poisoning. Call a doctor, organise transport for the affected participant(s) to hospital or back home. Notify the hotel and the primary client. Keep careful records.

Hotel problems (mis-booking, external noise, appalling service etc). Keep careful records (signed by other observers). Take it up – as soon as possible – with the hotel manager (not a minion). Refuse to sign the bill.

Report to your manager or employing company. Write a careful and itemised letter of complaint. Take legal advice where necessary.

Participant problems

These are common problems, with suggested courses of action:

Trainees drunk or fighting. Send them home. No arguments – get them off the course.

Problems with the primary client. Examples of this are: poor expectation-setting (the trainees not knowing why they have been sent on the course); punitive attitudes ('You'll go on this course or else'); participants swapped or brought onto the course at the last minute. Although such problems are not strictly your fault, you will still have to deal with them. You need to spend longer on the course set-up session to make sure that not only are the expectations corrected, but that reluctant learners realise that they will get value from the course. You can stop this from happening by keeping in regular contact with the primary client right up to the day before the course to make sure that there are no surprises. Always either have an extra couple of copies of the course documentation with you, or bring the master documentation with you so you can photocopy it when needed.

Accidents and acts of God

Common problems and suggested solutions are as follows:

No voice. Surprisingly this is not as awful as it might seem. It forces the trainer to be a facilitator and so involves the participants in the course much more than if you were talking at them. Explain (in a whisper) what has happened, elect a 'speak person', hand over your notes and let him or her get on with it, interceding with timely and accurate written observations where necessary. They will all be on your side!

Natural or man-made disaster. Take no chances with anyone's security – trainees first, trainer second. Get out. Record what happened (as soon as possible). Report back and get the trainees home safely. Make sure that loss records are made rapidly and accurately.

Handling difficult customers

Ah, that we lived in a perfect world! But, alas, we do not, and sooner or later we will come up against difficult customers. However, before putting your bullet-proof vests on – a general point: many of the disruptive behaviours have nothing to do with the trainer and are not the trainer's fault. This does not mean that these behaviours can be ignored – far from it, it is part of the trainer's duties to sort out problems – but it does mean that the trainer should not take the behaviours personally.

External causes of disruptive behaviour include: poor expectation- or objective-setting on the part of the trainee's manager; uncomfortable training surroundings which the trainer cannot influence; and outside distractions or worries beyond the trainer's control. The only way to handle these is to anticipate the worst and make sure that the objectives/expectations and so on are set by you, the trainer, on your course. As to external worries and distractions, show that you understand the circumstances but point out that this has nothing to do with the course.

The 'frightful four'

Let us look at the most common difficulties you can expect to encounter.

A few participants talk too much, not allowing others to contribute

This may be due to several causes:

▌ Enthusiasm on the part of the participant – this is good, but can limit the input of others. This person needs to be acknowledged and encouraged to listen to others.

❚ The participant feels overlooked or feels that his or her point of view has been ignored. This is not so good – maybe the trainer has been ignoring him, perhaps back at work his or her ideas and input have been ignored. This person may well become more aggressive if you attempt to keep him or her quiet. You could take him or her aside at break time and try to get to the bottom of what is happening.

Here are some strategies for coping with the garrulous:

❚ Interrupt (tactfully) with a question or summary statement.

❚ Ask this student to take notes and give them two minutes at the end of the discussion to summarise.

❚ When the talker pauses, rephrase their statement briefly and pass on to the next topic.

❚ Put this person in your 'blind spot' (usually right next to you, or at the front on the far right) and ignore some of his or her comments.

❚ Let the group handle it.

Several participants will not join in

There are many possible reasons for this: perhaps the withdrawn participants are the sort of people who like to evaluate before joining in, they may feel that they have nothing to contribute, or they may feel that there are more senior people present and that they have no right to speak.

Here are some strategies to cope with the quiet ones:

❚ Give them more time.

❚ Make eye contact with him or her while asking questions.

❚ Involve him or her in small group work and ask him or her to report on the group's findings.

❚ Ask questions directly of him or her.

❚ Phrase questions to appeal to his or her particular interests.

Participants have side conversations

This often happens on courses where all the participants know each other well and the course is dealing with how to solve existing work problems. Of course they want to talk about the effect of the course information on real life, and to a certain degree you should encourage this. The problem here is that the side conversation would add considerable value to the course if it were shared with everyone. If the side conversation seems to have nothing at all to do with the course it may be necessary to intervene to stop it – if it is distracting the rest of the participants, for example.

Here are some strategies to cope with the side conversations:

- Stop talking and wait for the side conversation to end.
- Stand behind the chatterers.
- Change the seating.
- Break up the chatterers.
- Ask a direct question of the chatterers.

Disagreement leading to confrontation

One participant adamantly disagrees with the rest of the group over a particular point and this develops into a real confrontation. Everyone is entitled to his or her own point of view. It is when a point of view becomes a 'rat-hole' that this stops the course from continuing. I have found it quite rare for a single participant to hold out for very long against the rest of the group. This does not mean that the individual has changed his or her mind, just that group pressure has stopped discussion.

Here are some strategies to cope with 'rat-holing':

- Let the group handle it.
- Get the participant to summarise his or her position.
- Change the subject.
- As a last resort, speak to the participant outside the course.

Where you have problems that interrupt the rest of the course you will need to lay down some ground rules or structure the exercises so that contributions from all are possible – for instance, try breaking the group into smaller teams where each person is more likely to contribute, or allocating specific tasks to specific people. Do not be too worried about the frightful four at the very beginning of the course, this behaviour may well be the result of the 'storming' phase of group formation.

Problems with individual participants

The know-it-all

These can be both a source of extra information and an exasperation. Most people are quite rightly proud of their knowledge and skills and want to share them with others. It is when it gets out of hand and the course seems to revolve solely around the expert that the trainer needs to intervene.

Try these strategies:

- Throw the question open to the rest of the course.
- Let the group handle it.
- Name the person to answer the questions.

The participant moves away from the subject

This often happens in discussion sessions where participants call on their experiences to illustrate points, or where particular worries and concerns only loosely involved with the subject under discussion are brought up.

Try these strategies:

- Remind the group of the subject under discussion.
- Ask the participant to hold his or her comments until later.

Participant moans about his or her management team

Very often the trainer is seen as a welcoming ear when the

participants' company is going through significant changes
– this is particularly so on management skills courses.
Whether the course is designed as a problem-solving
exercise or an exercise in gaining skills, moaning about
management will not move either objective forward. Since
the trainer very rarely has any power to change the way
the primary client runs the management team (as far as
the particular course is concerned), then nothing is gained
by allowing this to continue during the course sessions.
(It probably will go on at break times and after the course
anyway.)

Try these strategies:

▌ Get another participant to chair the discussion so that
you are not seen to be the arbitrator.

▌ Point out that the course is to help with the present,
not pie in the sky.

▌ Do not sympathise or join in.

Participant brings up a personal problem that only affects him or her

If the problem is pertinent and you can do something
about it, handle it there and then. If the problem is
unconnected to the course, acknowledge it and take it 'off
line' in the next break.

Participants are difficult to understand

This often happens when you have a mixed nationality
group where their mother tongue is not the same as yours
or the rest of the course's. It can also occur with non-
technological people on technology courses who simply
do not know the jargon. The trainer needs to interpret
where necessary and should try to take the course at a
slower speed. The basic rules are:

▌ Help the participants as much as possible.

▌ Rephrase and repeat questions and comments to make
them clear to everyone listening.

Personality clashes between participants

These are often inevitable, given that people are so different. The clashes are often about the speed at which people get things done – one person going too fast or slow for the other; or about the importance that people place on tasking and relationship behaviours – the task-master becoming impatient with the way others seem to take the tasks less seriously than he or she does, or vice versa.

The trainer is not there as a matchmaker but may have to intervene to keep the peace.

Try these strategies:

- Interrupt the quarrel with a direct question on the course topic under discussion.
- Bring another trainee into the discussion.
- Say that you feel personalities should be left aside for the purpose of the course.
- Never take sides.

Participant thinks 'I learned on the factory floor; so should everyone else'

This participant has nonetheless come onto the course, so they must have a reason for being there. Try these strategies:

- Ask for the benefit of his or her experience.
- Use this trainee as a second trainer.
- Do not antagonise!

Participant seems to dislike the trainer

Unless you have done something deliberately to antagonise this participant (which is unlikely), this may be an indication that the participant feels that he or she has not had his or her experience or knowledge recognised. Try this:

- Encourage the group to answer this trainee.
- Approach from a different viewpoint to reduce antagonism.

- At break time, try to find out if there is any unresolved conflict.
- Do not be pulled into an argument.

Persistent lateness

This drives me mad. I find this often happens when the training venue and the participants' offices are very near to each other. At break times, they wander back to their desks and get distracted. I try to make it a rule that no one goes back to his or her desk at break times, but this is hard to enforce. If lateness is persistent, try this:

- Start meticulously on time.
- Fine them.
- Ignore their late entry and let the rest of the group sort it out.

Two participants argue heatedly

If the argument is valid and contributes to the course, it is probably as well to try to take the heat out of it by summarising the differing viewpoints and integrating it into the module. If it is a personal argument you may need to do the following:

- Take control immediately.
- Point out that this argument is solving nothing.
- Take a vote and let it drop.

In brief

- Most course crises are avoidable with a little forethought and careful planning. I always work on a 'worst-case' basis that if it can go wrong it will, and legislate before the course for that. Fortunately crises are rare.
- The basic crisis-handling rules are: do not ignore it, do not panic, collect the facts, keep the course members informed, keep records, involve the participants if they

can help, cancel the course if the crisis is dire and keep communication clear.

■ Problems with individual participants need to be handled in their early stages, too. A direct approach (in private) will usually uncover the roots of the problem, and the very fact that you have taken notice sets the cure in process. Never ignore bad behaviour on the part of participants. The rest of the group is always on your side and will appreciate your taking control.

■ As for falling in love on the course? No problem – then or now.

8

Drawing the Course to a Close

This chapter looks at the final stages and aftermath of a course. How can you test whether the course has fulfilled both the course and personal expectations set at its start? How can you test whether the skills achieved are to a high enough standard? How can you bring a course to a successful close, leaving the participants with enthusiasm for the prospect of putting their new skills into practice? We also need to consider the course debriefing session: what should you do during the debriefing session, what are debriefing sessions for and what is the effect of this on future training?

Testing and assessing success

Why bother with testing? Surely any trainer worth his or her salt will know whether or not the course has been successful? True, but nonetheless even the best trainers need to make sure. What the trainees have learned while the charismatic trainer is there may not be retained in the absence of the trainer. A check is necessary.

There are several really good reasons for testing:

■ It is the final learning curve, reinforcing and putting into perspective what has been learned.

■ It is a 'safety net' allowing the trainer to see where extra effort may be needed, where back-up training is needed and where the course is successful or unsuccessful.

- It should make the testee feel successful.
- It proves to the paymasters that the trainer is prepared to stand by his skills and expertise.
- It can be used as a diagnostic tool to help with future job-planning and development.
- It gives the trainer a chance to reward the trainees.
- It points up the seriousness and value of the course.

A word of warning, however. If a test gives a sense of failure, or if a test is unfairly marked or presented it will do terrible harm – so much so that the course participant who fails a test will almost certainly have negative feelings about what they have learned, and will actively choose to forget even the things that they have succeeded in. Besides, if you make the course participants take a test that they fail – what does that say about your teaching methods?

You must therefore be very careful in selecting the type of test you use. Some tests are appropriate for behavioural/personal skills, some are appropriate for technical skills, and some are appropriate for intellectual skills.

A word about setting up tests

Present the test positively – none of the old schoolmaster behaviours ('this is good for you, unpleasant though it may be' or 'failure will result in detention' or 'your manager will be given the results').

- Present it as a challenge and a learning experience.
- Explain the test procedures carefully.
- Explain how the test will be marked.
- Try to de-stress the test atmosphere (even managing directors can quail at the thought of an 'exam').
- Give out the results privately.

Types of test

Testing can be done in a variety of ways: objective checking, written tests, oral testing, questionnaires, feedback during the course, feedback after the course, measurable results and observation on the course.

Objective checking

You will have collected the personal objectives at the beginning of the course and you will have made the course objectives clear, so the easiest way to check that these have been met is to ask the participants at the end of the course if they feel that they have met their objectives. You must also ask them to be explicit in how these objectives have been met, a simple yes is not enough proof!

Written tests

These can be as formal or informal as you like. In the main, written tests fall into three categories: open tests, half-open tests, closed tests.

Open tests are role plays, presentations etc where the behaviours of the testees are studied. There are no 'right or wrong' answers, the tester evaluates the performance to see if the behaviours are appropriate. The results can be very useful but extremely difficult to quantify. Ideally a final role play or presentation should be judged by an outsider, not the person who has given the course.

In half-open tests, the participant has to express in his or her own words the answers to the questions. No clues are given as to what the answer might be. Examples are:

- What important actions must a manager perform before an appraisal interview?
- What common fault is often made by a user when logging on?

As you can no doubt see, there are several possible answers to each question, and it is up to the person marking the test to decide which ones are correct. This is fine if the tester knows the parameters, but can lead to inaccuracy.

In closed tests the tester and the testee can see what the

answer might be, it is up to the testee to choose which response is most likely. For example:

Which command allows you to change your password?

a) COMPOSE

b) SIGN ON

c) PASSKEYS

The advantage of closed tests is that they are easily marked, accurate and fair – only one answer is correct. However, they can be extremely boring if they are badly composed or use terminology that has not been used during the course.

Oral testing

This can be done at any time during the course. Use a question and answer session as a summary to a course module, set up team quizzes, or ask them all to write down three things that they have learned from the session. Oral testing should occur throughout the course.

Questionnaires

Here I differentiate between written tests and questionnaires. The training questionnaire usually asks for feedback from each trainee on how the course has gone.

Overleaf is a simple questionnaire that can be used to test the effectiveness of the course and course logistics in general. Most questionnaires are fairly general, only asking for specifics in the comments column at the end. Questionnaires are useful if a general one is used for all the courses that a training department or company gives as it allows you to set minimal standards – but, of course, the questionnaires cannot be too specific in this case.

There are two schools of thought about when course questionnaires should be filled in: on the course, or after a period of time has passed and the new skills have been tried out in the real business world. Questionnaires filled in on the course will certainly check reactions to the course

SAMPLE QUESTIONNAIRE

Participant's Name: *Course Title:*   *Date:*

Please indicate your feelings about the course by selecting a grading for each question.

1=Unacceptable   2=Fair   3=Good   4=Excellent

1 How do you rate the training room?	1	2	3	4
2 How do you rate the course logistics?	1	2	3	4
3 How useful was the course?	1	2	3	4
4 How do you rate the course leader?	1	2	3	4
5 How do you rate the manual?	1	2	3	4
6 How did the equipment behave?	1	2	3	4
7 How do you rate the course content?	1	2	3	4
8 How do you rate the exercises?	1	2	3	4
9 What was the timing like?	1	2	3	4

10 Please grade each module in terms of effectiveness:

Module 1	1	2	3	4
Module 2	1	2	3	4
etc				

11 Please grade each speaker:

Felicity Ffarnes-Barnes	1	2	3	4
Anthony Smythe-Smith	1	2	3	4

12 Was there anything you would have left out of the course?

13 Was there anything you would have liked to include?

14 Are there any comments you would like to add?

itself, and this feedback reflects things like comfort, logistics and delivery methods and the trainer's performance skills. Whether it checks the efficiency of the learning process is a moot point. On the other hand, questionnaires filled in after a few weeks have passed will certainly check whether the new skills or information have been properly integrated. The trouble with this is two-fold: will the questionnaires really be returned to the right people? What external influences might affect the way the questionnaires are filled in?

I suggest a mixture of the two, where a brief questionnaire is filled in and collected on the course itself, and the manager or primary client provides a follow-up question-naire at a later date. Whatever happens, the trainer must see the results of the questionnaires, since this is the basis of any course amendment and improvement for the future.

Drawing the course to a successful close

There is an old Tony Hancock comedy sketch centred round a library book (a murder mystery), the last few pages of which have been torn out. This leads to extreme frustration on the part of the reader – Hancock – and a hilarious attempt to solve the mystery. Unless we take care to end our courses with a satisfactory denouement or ending, we are in the same position as a book with the final chapter missing.

A happy ending

These are the elements of a successful conclusion to a course: a course summary, a call to action, a link to the outside world, a contract to continue learning and a fond farewell.

The course summary

This is where all the course modules are drawn together. Even on short courses, the learning from earlier modules needs to be reinforced at the end of the course. Just as each module needs a summary, so does the entire course, particularly courses that last more than one day.

You can do this in two ways: trainer-led summaries or participant-led summaries. I like to use a mixture of both. In trainer-led summaries the trainer first goes through the course modules in the order in which they were covered. Here is an example:

AGENDA: INTRODUCTION TO PRESENTATIONS

1 Course introduction, objectives.

2 First presentations: 'Introducing Myself'. Diagnosis of performance, action lists.

3 'First Impressions'. Credibility and stance. The presenter's voice.

4 Presentation structure. Simple structure (Tell Tell Tell). The start – essential ingredients.

5 Presentation structure. The end – essential ingredients (second presentations).

6 Preparing presentations. Methodologies. Defining and clarifying the message. Speaker notes.

7 The audience – how they remember, what they forget, making the presentation memorable. Audience reactions.

8 Visuals – what – when – why – how. Visualising the message. Presenting visuals effectively.

9 Presentation structure – 'Horses for courses'.

10 After the presentation – question handling, handout materials from speaker notes.

11 Final presentations (second presentation).

12 Question and answer session (drawing all the information together), contract for change, initial course assessment.

13 Course ends.

This reminds the participants what the objectives were and what they have actually covered on the course. Then you point out how these link together with (in this case) preparation, research and relevance. (For example, see figure opposite.)

For each area, point out the importance of each facet and how it can be applied in the real world.

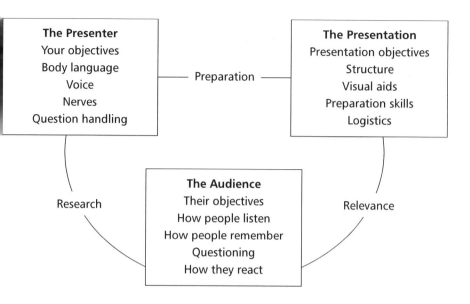

To launch a participant-led summary put up the agenda and then ask each participant to select a module to summarise, or show a linkage chart (as above) and ask participants to summarise what they have learned from each module. As with any feedback, this must be specific. Cloudy statements like 'I learned how important it is not to overload the audience with facts' are not clear enough. Ask questions like 'why?', 'what happens when overload occurs?', 'how can you avoid overload?' and so on. I also prepare a laminated summary card for each course which participants can use as a checklist after the course, since very few people indeed will carry their manuals around with them after the course.

The call to action

There should be two calls to action: a general one, that every participant can follow through, and a specific one addressed to each participant. Taking the example of a presentations course again, the general call might be something along the lines of: 'Try to take as many opportunities of making presentations over the next few weeks as you can. Use the presentation planners for each one'. The individual call to action might run like this: 'Fiona, keep using the vivid imagery that you use so well, but breathe more deeply and try the voice exercises for crispness'; 'Basil, your use of slides is excellent, but try not to have quite so many'.

This also acts as a link to the outside world where the participants will be thinking in terms of what they will be doing after the course, rather than just what they have done on the course. You also need to ask them what they will do differently as a result of what they have learned on the course.

The contract to continue learning

Very often you as trainer may not have the opportunity to follow up individual development after the course – a follow up workshop after a few months is a splendid chance to check how the skills are being used, but is not always possible. What can you do to encourage the participants to continue learning? You could encourage them to make a 'contract for learning' with other participants on the course, or fill in a 'contract for development' that they could share with their manager. An example of this is shown opposite.

The fond farewell

At the end of any social occasion there comes the time for the guests to leave. How do they know when to go? Is it written into the invitation, does the host announce that the last bus is leaving, do the guests just drift away in dribs and drabs?

Training courses need to end in three ways: with a bang, on time, and happily. The stop time for the training course should be clearly stated in the joining instructions and on the agenda. This time is sacrosanct. Never overrun. In fact if you can stop a few minutes early this is no bad thing. No matter how well the course has gone,

---

CONTRACT FOR FUTURE LEARNING

Over the next three months I undertake to do the following things when I make presentations:

. . . .

. . . .

. . . .

I would like feedback on the following skills:

. . . .

. . . .

. . . .

. . . .

Signed: Telephone/e-mail address

Witnessed: Telephone/e-mail address

Date (today):   Contact date:

---

overrunning really irritates participants and you will see feet beginning to point to the door, eyes looking at the clock, papers and manuals being purposefully gathered together and all the body language that suggests it is time to hit the road.

The last few moments of a course should be carefully structured. Here are some ideas:

- Use words like 'and finally…'; 'just before you go…'
- Go round the training room, shaking each person by the hand, thanking them for the energy they have put into the course, their inputs and their support.
- Give each participant your business card.
- Give out course certificates.
- End with a final anecdote or quote.

■ Award course prizes.

■ Restate the general call to action.

The debriefing session

This is vital and should be done as soon as possible after the course. You need to look at these areas: course logistics and venue, trainer performance, course structure and design, participant satisfaction (and the satisfaction of their managers), the relevance of the course to the business process and the satisfaction of the primary client.

Logistics

Go through your checklists (see Appendix B). If there is cause for complaint, follow the crisis handling instructions in Chapter 7 and be certain to check that all is as you want it to be before you use that venue again. Perhaps you need to brief the venue organisers and course administrators more carefully next time. Keep this record in case you need it in future.

Trainer performance

How did you feel the course went? Were you audible? Were you worried about any of your explanations or the ways you handled the course modules? Did you spend long enough on the introductions and course conclusion? Did you have any problems with particular participants? What would you do differently next time?

Course structure

Were any modules too long or too short? Did any need a different methodology? Were there enough breaks? What would you change?

Participant satisfaction

When you look through the feedback questionnaires are there any common trends? Were there any shortfalls in meeting course or individual objectives? Can the suggestions section be used to improve the course? Are there any requests for follow-up activities that will need to be organised?

Relevance

Were all the exercises, role plays and case studies real enough? Do they need updating? Do you need new examples? Have there been any changes in company behaviours that need to be taken into account for the next course?

Primary client satisfaction

Does the primary client want or need a report on how the course went? However, remember the caveat about reporting behind the participants' backs. How soon can you realistically do this? If you do it too soon, there will not be enough feedback; if you do it too late, the relevance of the feedback might be compromised.

Any course debriefing session is vital to the future running of the course or related courses. This is particularly so when you have just given a pilot course, since you would expect to make changes after testing the course out with a live audience. Even well established courses need to have a debriefing session each time they are run. It is easy to become stale after three or four course deliveries of material that you know well – the 'It must be Thursday, I'm telling that same joke again' syndrome. Careful debriefing allows you the chance of changing to a livelier methodology, updating your anecdotes and examples and keeping your own interest in the course at a level which allows you to deliver it with panache and enthusiasm.

In brief

▮ The end of a course needs to be as carefully planned as the start. Do not be tempted to hurry the ending or the participants will feel short-changed, even though they are glad to get away on time. You need to check that learning has taken place and that all objectives have been met.

▮ The end of the course should encourage the participants to take their new skills back to the workplace and use them as soon as possible, so even though you may be tired at this point, you need to energise the group for the last time.

▮ The course does not end when the participants have left. You need a debriefing session to evaluate what was good, what needs changing and what needs to be updated or actioned. The debriefing is your recipe for future success and to miss it out is a dangerous practice.

And finally...

Aristotle, one of the greatest teachers of all time, said this:

'What we have to learn to do, we learn by doing'.

It is *after* the course that the participants will learn by doing. It is the trainer's final duty to make this 'doing' as effective as possible.

Further Reading

ADAIR J. *Effective Decision-making*. London, Pan, 1985.

BELBIN R.M. *Management Teams*. London, Heinemann, 1981.

BIDDLE D. and EVENDEN R. *Human Aspects of Management*. London, Institute of Personnel Management, 1989.

BIRKENBIHL M. *Train the Trainer*. London, Chartwell Bratt, 1977.

BOLTON R. *People Skills*. Sydney, Prentice Hall, 1986.

BUZAN T. *Use Your Head*. London, BBC Publications, 1974.

BUZAN T. *Use Your Memory*. London, BBC Publications, 1986.

KIRKPATRICK A.L. *The Complete Public Speakers Manual*. London, Thorsons, 1986.

LEEDS D. *Powerspeak*. London, Piatkus, 1988.

LEWIS B. and PUCELIK F. *Magic of NLP Demystified*. Portland, Oregon, Metamorphous Press, 1990.

McCALLION M. *The Voice Book*. London, Faber and Faber, 1988.

MORRIS D. *Bodywatching*. London, Grafton, 1987.

SMITHIES D. *Speak in Public*. London, Unwin, 1985.

TURNER S. *Thorsons Guide to Public Speaking*. London, Thorsons, 1986.

WAINWRIGHT G.R. *Teach Yourself Body Language*. London, Hodder and Stoughton, 1985.

Appendix A: Sample Pre-course Questionnaire

PRE-COURSE QUESTIONNAIRE 'TRAINING THE TRAINER' COURSE

Please fill in the following questionnaire – this will really help us to tailor each course to your particular needs. We will use the 'case study' questions to design realistic role plays and the information about your training focus and experience to help us select the areas of training expertise on which we need to concentrate.

Thank you for your time and we look forward to seeing you on the course. Please return this questionnaire to your training manager by X.

Name:

Job title:

Manager:

Department/location:

Number of years in this position:

Previous jobs:

Previous training courses undertaken:

Training areas – subject or skill (in other words – what are you training people to do now):

Personal concerns about your role as a trainer:

Personal objectives for this course:

Any information you would like to add?

This section of the questionnaire is concerned with actual training situations you have encountered.

Think of the most unpleasant course you ever attended.

What sort of course was it and why were you on it?

. . . .

Describe the trainer:

. . . .

What were your expectations?

. . . .

Had you been trained by that trainer before?

. . . .

How long was the course?

. . . .

What were the difficulties that you had?

. . . .

How did you try to counter these?

. . . .

What could the trainer have done to make the course better?

. . . .

Why do you think that this course was so difficult?

. . . .

Think of the best course you have ever been on.

What sort of course was it?

. . . .

What was the trainer like?

. . . .

What were your expectations?

. . . .

Had you been trained by that trainer before?

. . . .

How long was the course?

. . . .

What were the best parts of the course?

. . . .

Why were these course modules so successful?

. . . .

How did the trainer make the course so good?

. . . .

Why do you think that this course was so good?

. . . .

You will need a colleague to help you fill in this part of the questionnaire.

Take a step back from yourself and try to answer these questions. When you have done your part, ask a colleague to answer the same questions on your behalf. (An extra page for this is included.)

(Your copy)

My four greatest training strengths are: (strengths here mean qualities like tenacity, judgement, friendliness, clarity in communication etc)

. . . .

My four main training skills are: (skills here mean qualities like technical expertise, product knowledge, market knowledge, etc)

. . . .

If I could change or enhance my training skills, these are the things I would like to look at:

. . . .

You will need a colleague to help you fill in this part of the questionnaire.

(Their copy)

X's greatest training strengths are:(strengths here mean qualities like tenacity, judgement, friendliness, clarity in communication etc)

. . . .

X's four main training skills are: (skills here mean qualities like technical expertise, product knowledge, market knowledge, etc)

. . . .

If X could change or enhance his (her) training skills, these are the things he (she) should look at:

. . . .

Appendix B: Venue Check-lists and Training Room Layout

General training room checklist (tick off when satisfied).

- Seating. Enough chairs with arms, enough room to stand by participants. Extra trainer's chairs (2)
- Lighting
- Manuals/handouts
- Equipment
  - Overhead projector
  - Screen
  - Slides
  - Flip chart/extra pads
  - Pens (any dried up?)
  - Blu-Tack
  - Camera/tripod
  - Monitor
  - Tapes
  - 35mm projector
  - Slides
  - Cables taped down and safe
- Ventilation, heating, air conditioning
- Water, glasses, mints
- Presentation area
  - Extraneous clutter
  - Clear walls/flip charts
  - My notes
  - Water/glass

- Clock/watch for timing
- Myself
  - All fastenings fastened?
  - Voice warmed up?
  - Preparation done?
  - Audience research done?
  - Glass of water at hand?
  - Somewhere to sit/stand/walk around
- 'Break-out' rooms
  - Seating
  - Light
  - Air/heat/ventilation
  - Flip chart/pens/pads.

Equipment and materials needed for 'Train the Trainer' course

For the Training Room:

- 10 chairs with arms
- 4 large tables (for the participants)
- 'Top table' for trainer's equipment
- 2 flip charts (each with 2 pads)
- 1 screen
- 1 overhead projector
- 1 video camera with microphones and stand
- Video lights and stands where necessary
- 1 television monitor with VHS video player
- 1 four-way plug extension
- Demonstration equipment (where applicable)
- 'Break-out' area with easy chairs and tables for participants (alternatively a separate break-out room)
- At least 4 three-pin sockets for basic training equipment
- Enough three-pin sockets to accommodate any demo equipment
- A side table for coffee pots and cups

■ Water/drinking glasses for each participant
■ Enough wall space to put up flip-chart sheets

For each Participant:

■ Training manual
■ Pencils
■ Notepaper (preferably to match the manual in size)
■ Large sheets A3 paper
■ Set of coloured felt pens
■ Index cards
■ Overhead foils (blank)
■ Pens for use with overhead projector
■ Video tape
■ Audio tape
■ Ruler
■ Name card
■ At least 6 flip-chart sheets
■ Set of flip-chart pens

General Equipment (to be shared):

■ Sweeties
■ Box for fines
■ Spare paper
■ Tape measure
■ Rubbish bin

Trainer's kit. I keep a small suitcase, permanently fitted out with the following:

■ Felt pens in black, red, blue, green (chisel-edged and as thick as you can manage)
■ Silver or gold stars
■ Spray glue
■ Pritt Stick

- Blu-Tack
- Sellotape
- Scissors
- Hole punch
- Stapler
- Overhead pens (medium and as many colours as possible – but not yellow!)
- Tippex
- Screwdriver
- Penknife
- Spare batteries
- Rubber
- Tape measure
- Business cards
- Sewing kit
- Matches
- Staple extractor
- Paper tissues
- Spare notepaper/pencils/pens
- Plain sticky labels
- Aspirin
- Red nail varnish
- Master training guide
- 'Amusement' audio tapes
- Tape recorder
- Tapes
- Stopwatch
- Portable computer
- Portable printer

TRAINING-ROOM LAYOUT

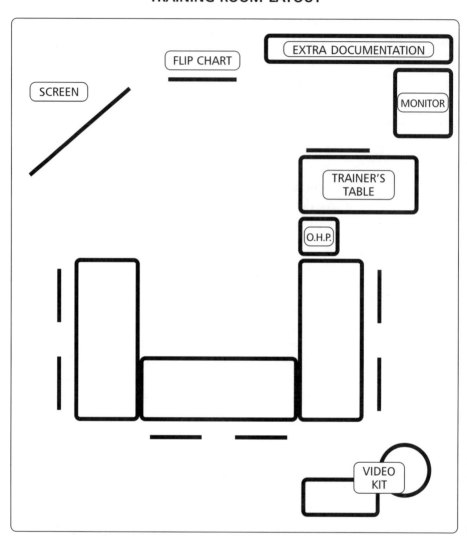

Plan the training room for the comfort of trainer and trainees. The U shape allows the trainer to move among the participants; the flip chart can be moved but should not clutter up the presentation area. The video kit is at the back and the monitor at the front so it can be easily wheeled into place. The overhead projector should not obscure the screen which should be visible from all positions.

Appendix C:
The Trainer's Voice

Projecting your voice without warming it up first is potentially damaging as well as embarrassing. Before you start a course, take a few moments with the following exercises. I find that if I do not warm my voice up first, I am croaky and likely to cough in the opening statements – not very efficient!

Voice exercises

- Straighten your back, relax your shoulders, stand tall.
- Take several really deep breaths, blowing the air out of your lungs as hard as you can.
- Warm up your lips with the following exercises:
  - Blow through loose lips, making a sound like a horse until your lips feel warm.
  - Make the sound mmmmmmmmmmmmmmmmmmmmm until your lips tickle.
  - Say 'muh buh muh buh muh buh muh buh muh buh muh buh muh buh muh buh'.
  - Say 'Puh buh muh 'Puh buh muh Puh buh muh Puh buh muh Puh buh muh'.
- Warm up your tongue with the following exercises:
  - Say 'Luh luh luh luh luh luh luh luh luh luh luh luh luh luh luh luh luh luh luh luh luh'.
  - Say ' Tuh guh kuh tuh guh kuh tuh guh kuh tuh guh kuh tuh guh kuh tuh guh kuh'.
- Now hum loudly up and down a scale and end with a loud 'aaaah'.

When you are training, always have a glass of water handy – never train with a dry mouth or throat, or your voice will end up hoarse and scratchy.

Projecting your voice

Even in quite small training rooms you need to project your voice more than you would in a normal conversation. This does not necessarily mean raising your voice or shouting, but is more like 'pushing' your voice out across the audience. The sounds that help you to do this are the plosives, the sounds that literally explode out of the mouth and carry further than other speech sounds.

The plosives are **P**, **B**, some **D** sounds, **T**, **hard G**, and **K** as in KiTTen, PaCKage, GrasP, TaG, BaD and so on. Putting slight stress on these plosives and articulating them really clearly (particularly at the ends of words) will give your speech enough crispness to allow it to be heard clearly at the back of the training room. Practise the verse below with a tape recorder until you are satisfied that your voice is crisp enough. You will be surprised how hard you have to work to make a significant difference.

Plosives exercise

Pretty Polly Peterkins sat in a tree.

Up popped a woodpecker.

Goodness me!

Tap went the woodpecker, Tap Tap Tap.

'Wait,' said Polly Peterkins, 'I want to take a nap.'

Little Polly Peterkins called for her cat.

'Kitty, kitty, come to me and sit upon my lap.'

Up came the kitty cat, climbing up the tree.

Naughty little pussy cat.

Goodness me!

Silly little woodpecker

R.I.P.

D

Appendix D: Visual Aids and Using the Overhead Projector

Visual Aids

A *good* visual aid will do at least one of these things:

- Help the audience to visualise abstract concepts: (charts/diagrams).
- Make the audience remember what you said: (eyecatching images, humour, colour).
- Show reality: (photographs, plans, maps, people's faces).
- Reinforce important and exact information: (numbers, exact quotes, financials).
- Link several complex ideas: (themes, build-up diagrams, headings).
- Compare information: (charts, competitive info. graphs, block diagrams).
- Summarise information: (short slogans, themes, calls to action).
- Introduce information: (name and title slides).
- Illustrate information: (artwork, photographs, mock-ups).
- Define information (glossaries, codes, close-ups).
- Inspire participants: (slogans, logos, calls to action).

IF IT DOES NOT – DO NOT USE IT.

A *bad* visual aid will do at least one of these things:

- Make abstract concepts even more abstract: (lots of words and symbols).

■ Cause the audience to forget what you have said: (no colour, no images, poor layout).

■ Distort reality: (poor graphics, unclear vocabulary, unclear syntax).

■ Misrepresent information: (mistakes, inaccurate and misleading numbers).

■ Confuse complex ideas: (no theme, over-complex diagrams, no headings).

■ Define badly: (jargon, unknown codes).

■ Bore participants: (pompous language, marketing speak, cliches).

■ Strain the eyes: (type too small, overcrowding, horrible colours).

■ Irritate participants: (messiness, poor placing on screen, lack of focus).

■ Give the audience headaches: (non-readability, small type, too much on screen).

■ Stop the audience listening: (too much complexity, no explanation of what it is about).

IF IT DOES ANY OF THESE – DO NOT USE IT.

For more detailed information, read Jacqui Gough's *Developing Learning Materials* in this series.

Using the overhead projector

WHAT A GOOD PRESENTER DOES	WHAT AN APPALLING PRESENTER DOES
Checks that the O/H is working and focused.	Arrives late, does not know whether there is an overhead.
Knows where the spare bulb is and how to replace it.	What!
Stands so the screen is not obstructed.	Stands directly in front of the screen.
Puts the slides onto the O/H carefully, aligned, and straight.	Who cares, and how do you do it anyway?
Looks briefly at the screen to check that all is OK.	Looks ONLY at the screen – after all, that is what reminds me of what to say, and who wants to look at the audience anyway?
Introduces complicated slides carefully, gesturing or pointing to the relevant sections.	Puts the slide up, starts talking and never points to the relevant parts at all.
Has all the slides in the correct order.	Drops the lot (but it does not matter, they were all higgledy piggledy anyway).
Has paper copies of the slides for anyone who wants them.	Such extravagance!
Has slides with a matching theme.	Uses any old slides from any old presentation.
Customises the slides to the audience as far as possible.	Waste of time! They will have what they're given.
Covers the O/H glass or switches off when not in use.	Leaves a bright blank screen to blind the audience.

Index